Teaching Young Children to Draw

Teaching Young Children to Draw

IMAGINATIVE APPROACHES TO REPRESENTATIONAL DRAWING

Grant Cooke
Deirdre Griffin
Maureen Cox

 Falmer Press

UK   The Falmer Press, 1 Gunpowder Square, London, EC4A 3DE
USA   The Falmer Press, Taylor & Francis Inc., 1900 Frost Road, Suite 101, Bristol, PA 19007

First published in 1998

A catalogue record for this book is available from the British Library

Library of Congress Cataloging-in-Publication Data are available on request

ISBN 0 7507 0653 8 paper

Design by Carla Turchini

Printed by Graphicraft Typesetters Ltd., Hong Kong

Contents

Acknowledgements

Figure 1.1 – Mogul drawing, reproduced with permission of the Victoria and Albert Museum, London.

Figure 1.2 – Japanese print, reproduced with permission of the British Museum, London.

Figure 1.4 – Rosemary Hill provided the Australian Aboriginal children's drawings. We also acknowledge the Warlpiri Media Association and thank the people of Yuendumu, Central Australia.

Illustration on page 31 – Grant Cooke drew the comic strip and this was first published in Cox, M.V., Cooke, G. and Griffin, D. (1995) Teaching Children to Draw in the Infants' School, *Journal of Art and Design Education*, **14**, 153-163.

We thank all the children and teachers involved in the development and evaluation of the 'negotiated drawing' lessons and the young artists whose work is reproduced in this book. In addition we are grateful to the following for their help: Annette Barrett, Kate Eames and Nikki Pitchford.

List of Figures and Tables

Why Teach Children to Draw?

Why Teach Children to Draw?

Children operate as 'artists' from a very early age using different materials for personal expression and as a way of exploring and making sense of the world in which they are growing up. This process of development needs to be supported by parents and teachers in a variety of different ways, ranging from encouraging free and imaginative expression to exploring the work of other artists and putting children in touch with conventions which will enable them to develop their confidence and skills in visual thinking, problem solving and drawing as a means of communication. For, as Norman Freeman (1980) emphasizes, 'children are not simply creatures expressing their essence through drawing, they are also novices who are learning how to draw'. This book is designed to provide teachers with an easily accessible and enjoyable approach to supporting children in their engagement with the drawing process.

Drawing as a way of making marks and controlling space on a flat surface is fundamental to all visual communication, whether for practical or artistic purposes. It can be the foundation for more imaginative picture making in art education, and has further importance as a medium in which children can record their observations in other areas of the curriculum and through which they can come to understand relationships and concepts important in a number of different subjects. A major problem for the teacher, and especially the non-specialist teacher, is how to go about the teaching of drawing. Since the subject has not attracted the same attention as some other aspects of the curriculum – such as reading, writing and number work – many teachers will have little or no training in how to teach drawing. Although most teachers provide opportunities for children to draw – as an art activity or as part of other project work – they have not necessarily considered the activity **in its own right** and how it might best be taught. It's not surprising then that many teachers feel at a loss and that over 60 per cent, according to a recent survey (Clement, 1994), feel the need for further inservice training if they are to teach the art curriculum. The lessons outlined in the main section of this book were originally devised as part of a professional development programme designed to introduce teachers working with infants to non-threatening ways of approaching the teaching of drawing.

Call for better provision and advice for art education in the UK was made in the early 1980s by, among others, the Calouste Gulbenkian Foundation (1982) and HM Inspectorate (DES, 1983). Even in 1990, however, HM Inspectorate was still lamenting the lack of any coherent and informed practice in primary schools. Introduction of the National Curriculum led to the teaching of art being taken more seriously. The National Curriculum Art Working Group was set up to identify and advise on the objectives of the teaching of art as a foundation subject for pupils between the ages of 5 to 14 years. Their report (DES, 1991) identified **drawing** as an activity central to all work in art and design and highlighted the importance of drawing from observation. Subsequently the National Curriculum for Art in England (DFE, 1995) has included a number of statements concerning the need for recording observations and an emphasis on drawing. For example, at Key Stage 1 (age 5–7 years) pupils should be taught to 'record what has been experienced, observed and imagined' and 'experiment with tools and techniques for drawing, etc.' (p.3). At Key Stage 2 (age 7–11 years) they should be taught to 'develop skills for recording from direct experience and imagination, and select and record from first-hand observation', 'record observations and ideas, and collect visual evidence and information, using a sketchbook' and 'experiment with and develop control of tools and techniques for drawing, etc.' (p.4).

Drawing can be used in many different ways, and drawing from an observed model is just one strand of art education. However, it is important because it introduces children to a convention of **representational image making** which involves careful looking, critical thinking and decision making in relation to drawing. It is a form of visual communication which is relatively easy to 'read', and has been used and understood by many different cultures at different times throughout history.

Representational Drawing

Representational modes of image making are often seen as essentially a Western art convention, associated with high points of achievement like the Renaissance, when clear visualization of three dimensional space became possible through the development of perspective. However, representational image making is also an important convention in World Art. Think of the correspondence with reality that one finds in Mogul miniatures and traditional Japanese prints, or in minor figures in ancient Egyptian wall paintings. There is a similar correspondence with reality in the huge hand-painted cinema hoardings in present day Madras and images in advertising which cross cultural boundaries. In these examples the artists have used different drawing techniques or 'depth clues' to suggest the spatial relationships between people and objects. They vary from what theorists would call 'single point of view perspective' and 'foreshortening' to flatter and more decorative indications of space using overlapping planes or 'parallel oblique perspective'. But what they have in common **is a recognizable connection between what we see in the picture and what we know from looking at the world around us.**

 1.1
'An Imperial Elephant', tinted Mogul drawing on paper, circa 1640: © Copyright Victoria and Albert Museum, London

In this Mogul miniature (figure 1.1) we can see elements of portraiture – the depiction of a particular, individual elephant. From this drawing we know the general shape of the animal and, because of the relative proportions of the mahout on its back, have some idea of its size. The sensitive rendition of the surface gives us some knowledge of the folds and textures of the elephant's skin. We also gain fairly detailed information about the ceremonial trappings worn by the animal through the decorative detail of the cloth on its back, and the ornate harness with its tassels and bells which holds the regalia in place. We know and recognize these things because there is a correspondence between the drawn image and observed reality.

The Japanese print of three women picking mulberry leaves to feed silkworms (figure 1.2) has a flatter more decorative quality than we would find in European art of the same period. The artist has used parallel oblique perspective which, unlike the Western form of

● 1.2
'Sericulture', Japanese print by Utamaro, circa 1798: © Copyright The British Museum, London

● 1.3
Contemporary hand-painted
cinema advertisement,
Madras

perspective developed in the Renaissance, does not have receding lines converging on a single vanishing point. However, we have little difficulty in deciphering much of what is happening in this frozen moment of communication between the two women who are reaching up and grasping branches of the mulberry tree and the woman passing below with two full baskets of leaves balanced across her right shoulder. As well as being aesthetically satisfying, the image conveys a great deal of recognizable information, even when viewed from the perspective of a different time and culture.

The contemporary artists from the South of India who produced this hand-painted advertisement (figure 1.3) are using representational imagery in a similar way to convey key aspects of the film's narrative – a dancer who continues her career despite having her leg amputated.

Of course there are vast differences between all these examples, and **great differences in the traditions and types of training that lie behind the work.** Over the centuries there has always been a degree of cross fertilization between different cultures, and the Mogul artist who drew the Imperial Elephant may well have been influenced by European artefacts in the same way that Western painters were at a later date influenced by the work of Japanese print makers. The hoarding painters in Madras are open to not only Indian and Western traditions of painting, but the influences of Indian and Western cinema, photography, and all that has become available world wide through new technologies.

Many important culturally based meanings will only be truly accessible to the particular audience for whom the artwork was produced. However, the artists responsible for these representational images have used and developed schema in which there is some visual correspondence between the shapes created and observed aspects of reality. This is primarily a process of matching linear shapes with outlines of people or objects and is a form of representation which makes some obvious meanings readily accessible to viewers across time and cultures.

Cultural Influences

All our ideas are to a large extent shaped by the culture in which we grow up, and none of us develops in a cultural vacuum. We are all immersed in and influenced by the kinds of images we see around us – on film and television, in the street and in shops and galleries, in books and magazines. Even if we are not explicitly taught how to produce a particular image, what we do produce may still be influenced by the images we have been exposed to. When we study children in different cultures we can see that even though there may be individual variation in the images they create there is also a strong influence of the particular culture they are developing in (Wilson, 1985).

In some traditional cultures, in which adults produce formal designs but no representational artwork, the children may likewise create patterns but no representational pictorial forms (Fortes 1940, 1981; Alland, 1983). In other cultures where adult art is representational, the style of images produced by adults will influence the way that children draw. For example, a study in Bali (Belo, 1955) showed that when drawing the human figure the children adopted the style of the figures in shadow puppet plays popular in that culture. In

Australia, young Warlpiri children listen to adults' stories and see the accompanying illustrations they draw in the sand. When the children themselves draw, they reproduce the curved horse-shoe shape that adults use to denote a human figure; when they go to the community's nursery school, they begin to draw typically 'westernized' versions of the human figure (Cox, 1993; Cox and Hill, 1996). In both styles of drawing the children make developmental changes – moving from simplified to more complex versions – and they will use both styles in the same picture (see figure 1.4).

● **1.4**
Warlpiri children's drawings

British children, growing up in today's post-modernist world, can contextualize their own art work within a broad range of images from other cultures, constantly being expanded by advances in technology. They have access to many conventions and are soon able to 'pick and mix' in a way that was not open to previous generations. This provides teachers and children alike with opportunities to enjoy what Salman Rushdie (1990) refers to as rejoicing in our 'mongrelization', for 'Melange, hotch-potch, a bit of this and a bit of that is how newness enters the world'.

Very early on children recognize representational images as an important cultural convention. Before they have developed the ability to read written text, they are familiar with book illustrations, comics and advertising, and develop a sophisticated ability to 'read' and extrapolate from not only whole pictures, but parts of an image, guessing what the rest of the drawing might be. They realize the power of these conventions and the advantages of having control over them themselves. (For a fuller account of the development of children's drawings, see Cox, 1992.)

Learning Through and About Drawing

Although sometimes dismissed as mere 'scribbling' the drawings of young children are purposeful and encapsulate important learning. In many ways these are the equivalent of children's 'role-play', and might be said to have the same relationship to formal art work that make-believe play has to drama. Harnessing the child's ability to experiment with different roles in drama involves teacher interventions within a facilitating structure, with a gradual referencing of the cultural conventions that underpin drama as an art form. We would suggest that the equivalent is true in terms of children's mark making, with the teacher gradually introducing children to ways of thinking and organizing their drawing which allow them to assume more responsibility for their own development. What we therefore need to consider is the kind of teacher interventions that will support young children into new understandings about the drawing process and enable them to make their own informed decisions as they develop as artists.

Although we can argue about what it means to 'teach' , to 'educate', to 'learn', and so on, most of us accept that we should do more than simply provide children with the materials and an interesting topic for their artwork. The transmission of knowledge and skill between people of the same generation and from one generation to the next allows for the possibility of rapid learning; without this cultural transmission, each generation would be condemned to re-create the wheel. One psychologist who set considerable store by the importance of cultural transmission was Lev Vygotsky (1934/1962). He argued that as early humans developed more technologically sophisticated tools to cope with the physical environment they also developed ways of cooperating and communicating. Examples of these 'psychological tools' are speech, writing, systems of number and picture making. Vygotsky believed that children come to grips with these systems within a **social context** before they begin to use them independently for themselves. Although they may pick up some things by simple observation as well as through their own experience there is much which can be achieved by tuition.

When a child is confronted with a task or a problem there are many aspects to it and many potential routes to a solution; the child may not know that many of these are irrelevant or not viable. Without necessarily **telling** the child the answer an 'expert' adult can guide the child towards a potential solution. Thus, the adult's role is to help the child to structure the way she thinks about the problem and guide her towards a solution. In this way, the child's own knowledge and skill develops rapidly since she may discover a more sophisticated solution than she would otherwise achieve on her own. Vygotsky used the term 'zone of proximal development' to refer to this difference between what the child can achieve on her own and what she can achieve with tuition from others.

Drawing is used by both professional adults and children in many different ways. It is used to explore and play with ideas, to find solutions to problems and to communicate information and ideas to others in simple forms like diagrams and within more complex conventions like architects' drawings. Shapes are made for their own sake, with the artist taking delight in pattern, colour and texture and engaging with the more formalist qualities of the medium. Drawing is used to tell stories and to illustrate or enhance narrative. It can be used to encapsulate sound and movement, with the child taking physical pleasure in acting with the medium as a story is dramatized, or the comic strip artist depicting sound effects as the super hero or heroine vanquishes the foe.

In school, representational drawing can provide a basis for more freely expressive art work and many examples of this approach with young children are outlined in the lesson descriptions included in this book. Drawing from observation provides a flexible set of conventions for the language of visual representation, which children are required to bring into play in relation to recording, analysis and planning in other curriculum areas such as science, maths and design technology. Drawing is used in relation to first-hand experience as the child makes a visual record of the weekly growth of a broad bean plant in a jar in the classroom. It is used in relation to secondary sources as the child refers to photographs in making a drawing of an endangered species of animal. A process like 'negotiated drawing' uses and reinforces work to do with recognition of shape in maths. Drawing becomes a tool for problem solving and design when young children are set an exercise like 'show how to rescue this fat Father Christmas who is stuck in a chimney'.

Representational drawing can also become part of a process of symbolization in which the image created holds meanings beyond the form of the object depicted. The same is true of representational images in paintings. For example, Van Gogh's well-known painting of a chair is not just **any** chair, but a chair that has special meaning because of its psychological value and location within the room in which it belonged. The wolf in the illustration of Little Red Riding Hood is not just **any** wolf, but the monster that has just devoured a grandmother. When a child makes a drawing of her bedroom, the objects drawn are not just toys but carry the value of what they mean to the child who knows, owns and plays with them.

This book sets out to provide a flexible and enjoyable programme for empowering young children to draw from observation, and does not involve the kind of rote drawing exercises associated with early twentieth-century art education. It is based on the premise that children gain from insights into the ways in which adult artists set about organizing their graphic descriptions and devising their own individual strategies for representational drawing.

The Artist as Role-model

The National Curriculum places emphasis on the need to make connections between the children's own artwork and that of other artists. Many teachers will bring artefacts and reproductions into the classroom and provide opportunities for children to discuss the work of both Western and non-Western artists. This is an important aspect of art education, but the focus tends to be on the finished image rather than the process of constructing the image.

Some schools are in the fortunate position to be able to invite artists into the classroom to work with children. Such 'artists in residence' schemes enable children to observe the **process** of producing a painting or drawing rather than seeing only the finished product. Through this experience they can get some idea about the difficulties and problem-solving aspects of the picture-making task as well as gain some knowledge of the materials and graphic devices artists use. They not only see adult artists in action, but they can discuss with them what their aims are and how they are trying to achieve them. They may also come to understand that picture-making is not always easy even for an 'expert'– there may be many 'stops and starts' and alterations – so they should not be discouraged when they themselves find the task difficult.

If a school is not fortunate enough to be able to have artists in residence there is a great deal that non-specialist class teachers can do by becoming actively engaged in the process of drawing, providing an important adult role-model for the children. Children are more likely to become interested in activities that adults themselves are interested in, enthusiastic about and engaged in. However, children rarely have the opportunity to see their teacher as 'artist' and many teachers explicitly distance themselves from this role by claiming that they cannot draw. But refined art skills are not necessary for teachers to productively engage in drawing with children, and the process of 'negotiated drawing' outlined in this book can easily become part of the normal repertoire of teaching strategies employed by any class teacher. This approach is **not** based on the notion that the teacher is an 'expert' who is showing the children a 'correct' way to draw. On the contrary, the children tell the teacher what to do, and the marks she makes on the board become a focus for discussion and a way of opening up and making explicit the decision-making process involved in representational drawing.

A research study carried out by Elizabeth Pemberton and Keith Nelson (1987) with pre-school children compared a group of children who drew with the encouragement of an adult, and another group who were engaged in mutual drawing sessions **with** an adult artist. Subsequently they noted an improvement in the drawings of the second group. The authors suggest that the children benefited from seeing more complex images than they themselves could produce, but in addition, it was the **interactive experience of the process** which resulted in the improvement in their representational skills.

Ernst Gombrich (1960) draws attention to the way that the work of adult artists is based on understandings derived from the work of others, and goes so far as to suggest that without schema and knowledge of a variety of pictorial devices no picture would be possible. We believe that young children can be introduced to some basic conventions for constructing graphic representations in a structured but non-impositional way. However, this book is not about teaching a technique that encourages children simply to enlarge their vocabulary of schema through diagrammatic formulas. It is about empowering children in a much more fundamental way, **by introducing them to a process of perceptual analysis that can lead to a continuous modification and development of representational schema.**

Different Views about Art Education

Art educators, especially those involved in teacher training, hold very particular views on how children should be encouraged to produce their own artwork. There are some who adhere to a school of thought rooted in the notion that child art should be allowed to develop naturally with little interference from adults apart from encouragement. The process of 'negotiated drawing' has been criticized because it is interventionist and focuses on a mode of representation which is seen as a Western, ethnocentric approach. We have already drawn attention to some of the similarities between representational art from different cultures, and would stress that within our approach this mode of realism is contextualized within other forms of imaginative drawing, with child-generated drawing structures.

Many teachers worry that giving tuition in how to draw is simply too prescriptive. Their concern is that drawing, and indeed all art work, should be largely concerned with the child's own imaginative expression and that adult interference will be inhibiting or even damaging. This concern about the possible adverse influence of adults is perhaps a reaction to the very formal art curricula developed in the late nineteenth and early twentieth centuries. The art educator Viktor Löwenfeld (1957) appealed to teachers, 'Don't impose your own image on a child. Never give the work of one child as an example to another. Never let a child copy anything.'

Of course, we would not wish to advocate an approach to drawing that simply consists of a diet of copying. But even if we did allow children to copy an image, would they in fact produce carbon copies of the original? David Pariser (1979) made a free-hand copy of Dürer's 'Rhinoceros' woodcut and enlarged it to 5 ft by 3 ft (1.5m x 0.9m) so that his pupils could more easily see all the rich graphic devices used to obtain effects of density, pattern, and so on. After he had told the children Kipling's story of *How the Rhinoceros Got his Skin*, he urged them to use his picture as an aid when illustrating their chosen story. In fact, there was great diversity in the children's pictures, with some concentrating on the principal features of the animal itself and others investigating the graphic devices such as use of parallel lines, cross-hatching and stippling. So, even though the task was essentially a copying one it did not lead to the production of stereotyped images as Löwenfeld might have feared. Copying in this context, as Pariser agues, is simply a first step but children must go on to use it for their own purposes, as indeed they did.

Methods Advocated in this Book

The strategies described in this book are not difficult to employ. They can be adopted and adapted by teachers to enable young children to become aware of the range of different options which they have when they engage in drawing. They focus on recognizing shapes and relationships and the decision making process involved in finding ways of recording these in two dimensions. This approach has grown out of many years spent working in classrooms with infants and their teachers, and is designed to cater for the needs of class teachers who may lack confidence in their own drawing skills. Sadly, insecurity of this kind means that many teachers underestimate the ability they have to help young children learn to draw with greater accuracy and confidence. We would therefore like to stress that 'negotiated drawing' centres on the teacher's ability to engage with young children, and use the questioning skills which are at the heart of good pedagogy, rather than on his or her own personal drawing skills.

The ways of working outlined in this book have been the subject of a research project in which both a specialist art teacher and a supply teacher with no formal art training employed the same methodology in a sequence of drawing sessions with full classes of infants. The details and results of this project are given in the last section of the book. They indicate the effectiveness of this method in engaging children in the drawing process in ways that made a significant contribution to their development in this area of the art curriculum. Essentially it embodies a holistic approach to education, in which drawing is contextualized and integrated with other curriculum activities including drama, imaginative story building and problem solving. It allows for vital links to be made between different subject areas of the curriculum, and provides for language development in its broadest sense, with children being encouraged to find physical, verbal and visual ways of describing and interpreting shape and spatial relationships. Through careful questioning on the teacher's part it engages children at a cognitive level, progressively making specific as well as general language demands of a high order. It does not involve imposition, or the premature teaching of complex conventions such as 'perspective drawing' or 'tonal relationships' which are associated with the work of more mature artists. In essence, it is designed to help teachers and children to **engage together** with the process of drawing as an enjoyable activity, and to guard against the development of notions like 'I can't draw!'.

Over the years we have tried various ways of empowering young children to learn through, and gain satisfaction from, drawing from observation. The strategy that came to be termed 'negotiated drawing' was developed because we found that it motivated the children and seemed to promote much richer and more detailed drawings. Infants engaged with interest in both the whole class activity and individual drawing tasks, and seemed to gain a greater sense of achievement and self-esteem through their work. They developed in confidence because they rapidly became aware that they were grasping and using a drawing convention they recognized because of the way that it is used in their surrounding culture. These subjective judgements have been reinforced by research findings, which also indicate that successfully employing 'negotiated drawing' does not depend on the teacher concerned having a specialist art education or sophisticated drawing skills.

Children need a rich and varied curriculum in art that provides for many different kinds of experience. 'Negotiated drawing' is a useful aid to development in just one strand of this, but it also provides an introduction to careful questioning of what we can see in the world around us and how this can be represented in both verbal and visual language.

The lessons outlined in the following sections of this book are designed to be borrowed and adapted to meet the needs of different groups of children and their teachers. Many of them have been used by curriculum leaders in primary schools as the focus for professional development days. We hope that all those who engage in the process of 'negotiated drawing' have as much fun as we have had drawing and talking with infants, and discussing their pictures with them.

What Do We Mean by 'Negotiated Drawing'?

It is common for teachers to set up an object for children to draw from observation, but the children are often given little guidance about how to engage in the process of making a representational drawing. If children show reluctance about starting the exercise, or complain that they can't draw, the teacher often encourages them 'to look very carefully' or 'look harder'. The skilful artist will know intuitively 'how to look' and then 'how to draw', although of course not all artists will look or indeed draw in the same way. But, what is the **child** or 'novice' to make of such advice? The art educator, Betty Edwards (1979 and 1986) realized how vague and unhelpful it was when she told her students to look at a still-life scene and to draw exactly what they saw. The students were in despair, saying, 'I **am** looking but I can't draw it.'

If children are to gain in confidence in how to observe an object and then to make a representational drawing, we must make this process explicit and this is what the teacher sets out to do in negotiating a drawing **with** the children. Essentially the process involves the teacher focusing the children's attention on an object and encouraging them to observe and describe its constituent shapes, their proportions and the way they interrelate. It is the teacher who undertakes the drawing, using a board so that the image which is constructed is large enough for all to see and marks can easily be erased.

The intention behind the exercise is that the children gain insight into the process of drawing through being helped to formulate a relationship between the object and the marks which the teacher makes on the board. The teacher presents an important role model – the adult 'artist'. But at the same time there is something else at play which provides a sense of fun. A reversal of normal classroom relationships is brought about because the children are given responsibility for 'telling the teacher what to do' and 'correcting her mistakes'!

- The children are seated so that they **all have approximately the same view of the object** chosen for the lesson and **the board on which the teacher is going to draw.**
- The exercise begins with the teacher and children **discussing the object as a whole** – its function, shape, design values, whether or not they are familiar with objects of this kind, etc.
- The teacher asks the children to **help her to draw this mutually observed object by providing her with clear verbal instructions.**
- As she begins the drawing, the teacher **makes deliberate errors of judgement involving shape, scale, placement and orientation.**
- The children are encouraged **to point out inaccuracies in the teacher's drawing.** These are discussed, with the children amending their 'instructions' if this was the cause.
- The teacher's drawing becomes a **focus for language development** as the children make judgements and struggle to articulate what they think should be drawn next, describe shapes, and discuss matters of scale, direction and orientation.
- **The drawing on the board is not completed,** with the exercise lasting only a sufficient time to serve its purpose.
- Before the children begin their own drawings, **the object which they have been using as a model is contextualized within a story or imaginative drama.**

- **The teacher's drawing is rubbed from the board** so that the children do not copy from this when they start their drawings.
- The **object is left for the children to refer to** as they make their pictures.

Traditionally in art lessons, interactions between the teacher and children tend to be conducted on a one-to-one basis as the teacher moves round the room from table to table. However, with often over thirty children in the class this can be a slow process, in which many children who have not been able to engage with the task are left to their own devices until the teacher has time to give them attention. Negotiated drawing can be a **whole class activity** in which the teacher and children embark on the drawing process together, without anyone being left out. They are focused into the task by the teacher in a way which makes the exercise seem fun, and a skilful teacher can make sure that all members of the class are actively engaged and contribute to the work regardless of their drawing ability, or the degree to which they are able to give precise verbal instructions. This can be a great advantage in a classroom in which there are bilingual learners. It also means that every child in the group will have some notion of how to begin their own personal drawing later in the lesson, allowing the teacher much more time with those who require some extra help.

When the children become familiar with negotiated drawing, and start to accommodate the processes involved to do with recognition of shapes and forming a clear relationship between these and their mark making, there is no longer a need to begin drawing lessons in this way. After a sequence of six or more lessons involving negotiated drawing, many children will be ready to make a representational image with little help from their teacher. This means that this approach can be set aside, and just re-visited again when the need emerges. But starting a drawing programme in this way means that even when the teacher is helping children on an individual basis, both teacher and child have common reference points which can be very useful. Within this context, 'reminder' questions like 'Look carefully ... what shapes can you see? Which shape are you going to choose to start your drawing?' make a different kind of sense for the children.

Examples of Lessons Using Negotiated Drawing

Examples of Lessons Using Negotiated Drawing

In this section of the book a selection of lessons in which negotiated drawing is used are outlined to provide models for teachers to adapt, or adopt, in order to meet the needs of their own particular classes.

A degree of repetition is involved in the description of lessons so that each account stands on its own, with reminders about key aspects of the process for teachers who are not used to working in this way. There are, however, differences in emphasis in the commentary on each lesson and there is an indication of this at the start of each account. For example, in some lessons greater emphasis is placed on the way in which a context for the children's own drawings is developed because of the drama techniques involved.

The lessons that have been selected were all originally delivered as part of a structured drawing programme for classes of infants who had one drawing session a week for a period of six to ten weeks. In other words, there was a special emphasis on representational drawing which lasted for at least half a term so that the children had a real chance to develop skills and understandings, and accommodate these into their repertoire.

The collection of lessons outlined in this section of the book, and the briefer examples provided later, are not presented in any chronological order. They are borrowed from work undertaken with children in Reception classes and Years 1 and 2 in a range of different schools. This means that teachers who want to devise a drawing programme for their class are in a position in which they can 'pick and mix'!

We would advise teachers to select the lessons which best fit in with work the children will be undertaking in other curriculum areas, or the objects and ideas you think will appeal to your class. In some cases your choice will be limited by how easily you can get hold of particular objects. However, you will probably find that when you can't get hold of something described in one of the examples you will find another 'real object' which is just as interesting to draw, and have great fun devising a story or drama in which to contextualize it for the children!

All full accounts of lessons follow the same three-stage format – negotiated drawing, developing an imaginative context, and the children making their own drawings. However, some of the brief examples are of lessons with children who had reached a point at which the first stage had become unnecessary as they were ready to engage in a drawing from observation without this kind of assistance from their teacher.

Reproductions of children's drawings are included to provide examples of the kind of work children have produced as a result of this approach to teaching young children to draw.

The Magic Vacuum Cleaner

This lesson was designed as an introduction to 'negotiated drawing' and has been successfully employed as the first in a sequence of drawing lessons with Reception classes and children in Year 1. In this account, illustrations are used to clarify key aspects of the process of negotiated drawing to help the reader visualize what this means in practice.

Real Object

An old cylinder vacuum cleaner

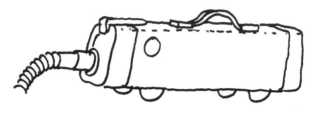

① Negotiated Drawing

The teacher has decided that she would like the class to draw a vacuum cleaner, and in preparation for the lesson has thought of a way in which she can build a humorous story around this piece of domestic equipment!

Organizing the workspace

BOARD
REAL VACUUM CLEANER
MAKE SURE THIS ANGLE IS NOT TOO WIDE SO THAT CHILDREN HAVE A SIMILAR VIEW OF OBJECT TO BE DRAWN
CHILDREN
TEACHER
LEAVE SPACE SO THAT TEACHER CAN WALK IN FRONT AND SEE CHILDREN'S POINT OF VIEW.

Before the start of the session the teacher works out how the children will need to be seated. The vacuum cleaner will have to be placed carefully in relation to the board on which the teacher is going to make her drawing, and she needs to ensure that all the children have a **similar view of the object.**

Initial discussion

When the class are all sitting where they can see the object she has chosen for the lesson, the teacher begins to discuss with the children how the vacuum cleaner works. The children make comparisons between this object and the vacuum cleaners many of them have in their own homes.

Teacher asks the children to help her draw the vacuum cleaner

Teacher makes mistakes

The children suggest that the shape of the 'front' of the vacuum cleaner is square. The teacher draws a circle and then a triangle making obvious 'silly mistakes' for the children to correct. The children are concentrating, but there are ripples of laughter – it's fun to be able to correct the teacher!

EVENTUALLY THE TEACHER DRAWS A SQUARE

THE TEACHER ERASES THE SQUARE   THEN · · ·

The children are beginning to compare the proportions of the drawn rectangle with the proportions on the front of the actual object. Eventually the teacher draws a rectangle that is close to the proportions of the rectangular 'front' of the vacuum cleaner.

Teacher   So you agree that this is near enough..? If you don't, you can make it better when you do your own drawings...

The teacher checks that most children are satisfied with the correlation between object and image, but makes it clear that they can reassess this in their own drawings.

The children decide that the next part that they would like to draw is the handle.

The children eventually decide that the curve has to be smaller and touch the top line of the rectangle, slightly to one side as it is on the vacuum cleaner. The teacher follows the children's instructions and the drawing is amended several times. Once the class are happy with the marks which the teacher has made on the board, she brings this section of the lesson to a close. The teacher's drawing on the board is left unfinished because it has already served its purpose.

The purpose of the teacher's drawing is to provide a FOCUS that enables the children to think about drawing as a process that involves careful looking and decision making. It is not a copying exercise, so she will wipe her drawing off the board before the children start to draw.

❷ Developing the Context

Now the teacher begins to tell a story that is designed to fuel interest in the vacuum cleaner, and form an imaginative basis for the drawings the children will be asked to do in the final section of the lesson. It is therefore **the aspects of children's drawing which are concerned with imagination and memory that have become the focus for this section of the lesson.**

Teacher	This is a magic vacuum cleaner...It's very powerful, and we are going to take it for a walk... But first of all, I'd like you to tell me some of the things that you see when you go for a walk...The sort of things you might see in a street...
Children	Shops
Teacher	What's in the shops?
Child	Sweets
Child	A person taking a dog for a walk
Child	A bus

The teacher has a large sheet of paper on her knee, and each time the children make a new suggestion she ritualistically tears off a small piece and lets it flutter to the floor. The children are intrigued, wondering why their teacher is littering the floor with scraps of paper! When she has elicited a suggestion from each child in the group, the teacher moves the story on.

Teacher	Now I told you that this was a magic vacuum cleaner... and it's very powerful...[She switches on the noisy machine, and starts sucking up the small scraps of paper.] It sweeps up all the sweets...and the man taking his dog for a walk...and the bus with all the passengers in it...!

There is laughter in the room as each child hears his or her suggestion being incorporated into the story, and they imagine the magic vacuum cleaner sweeping away the entire neighbourhood.

③ The Children Make Their Own Drawings

When the story comes to an end, the teacher wipes her drawing of the vacuum cleaner off the board. The children are now asked to make a drawing of themselves going for a walk with their own magic vacuum cleaner, and show all the different things that get swept away. The real vacuum cleaner is left on the table so that children can refer to this in the course of making their drawings.

As the children start their individual drawings, the teacher moves around the tables offering support where necessary. The children are encouraged to talk about their pictures, and explain all the rich detail of what is happening.

The completed drawings have become a 'holding form' for the children's stories and can lead to more language work as the pictures are shown to others, including adults at home. Later, some children may want to write down their story.

A – An exceptionally sophisticated drawing by a 6-year-old in which the figures have been drawn in profile and she has used 'occlusion' to indicate what is happening inside the supermarket and the figure mounting the stairs. Note the child's confidence in depicting the complex details of the vacuum cleaner, the shoes worn by the figure in the foreground and the shopping carried by the figure in the supermarket.

B – Although the simple figures indicate that the boy who made this picture is one of the less able children in the Year 1 class, the vacuum cleaner is depicted with considerable accuracy and attention to detail.

C and **D** – Both these children have depicted the vacuum cleaner within a rich imaginative context. In **C** the switch, handle and other details of the vacuum cleaner are confidently drawn with a variety of figures facing in different directions. In **D** the child has experienced some difficulties with 'occlusion' – the legs of the figure can be seen through the vacuum cleaner – but we can clearly see key elements of the imaginative story with the dog, tree and bird about to be sucked into the vacuum cleaner.

● **2.1**
'Going for a Walk with the Magic Vacuum Cleaner' – Drawings A, B, C and D are by children in Year 1, and E and F by members of a Reception class

Super market · Stairs

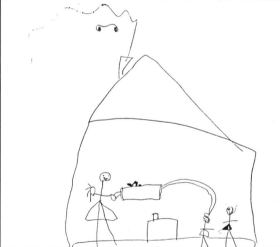

E and F – The same lesson was undertaken with the class of 5-year-olds who produced these drawings. Note how the child who produced drawing F has managed to rotate the house and tree as they are sucked into the machine.

The Dancing Skeleton

An account of a lesson which was originally devised for a class of infants who had been looking at bones, and was designed to tie in with some drama relating to a series of amusing books about a family of skeletons. The lesson is described with commentary that reinforces key aspects of the negotiated drawing process.

Real Object

A 'life-size' inflatable skeleton

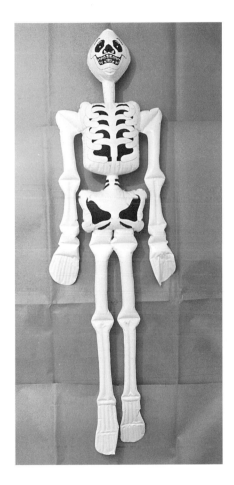

❶ Negotiated Drawing

The teacher suspends the inflated skeleton in a prominent position close to the drawing board. The class are then asked to sit in a way which, as far as possible, enables them all to have a similar view of the front of the skeleton.

Teacher   Can you help me draw this skeleton? You'll need to give
           me very clear instructions so I know exactly what to
           do... Should I start at the head or body?

*Sometimes where to start the drawing is left completely up to the
children, but in this case the teacher has a good reason for limiting
the choice to 'head' or 'body'. A clear example is needed at the start
of the exercise and, given an open choice, a child sitting at the front
might choose something too small like the skeleton's toes! It's
important that the teacher 'asks' rather than 'tells' so that there is a
real sense that it is the children who are 'in charge', but this means
thinking carefully about the questions posed.*

Child   Head!
Teacher   What SHAPE is the head?
Child   A circle

*In actual fact it is not a perfect circle, but the teacher takes the
child's suggestion and draws a circle near the bottom of the board.*

Child   It's too low!
Teacher   [asking all the class] What's wrong with that?
Child   There's no room for the body.

*This OBVIOUS MISTAKE made by the teacher demonstrates for
the children that initial marks need to be carefully placed. Planning
is necessary to allow space for the whole object to be represented in
the drawing.*

The teacher now rubs out the original circle and draws a very large
circle near the top of the board, erasing this when the children say
that it is too big, and replacing it with a smaller circle.

Teacher   [pointing to the head of the skeleton] Is this a
           proper circle?

A short discussion ensues in which different children compare the
shape of the skeleton's head with the shape 'oval' and 'an egg'.
Following new advice from the children, the teacher now narrows
the lower part of the shape on the board which represents the skull.

Teacher   I don't want to draw in the place where the eyes go, and
              the teeth now... When you do *your* drawings you can
              add all those things.

*The teacher judges that these features printed on the surface of the
inflatable skeleton are too easy, and wants to move on to other parts
of the body.*

The children decide that the neck of the skeleton should be added to
the drawing.

Next the children give the teacher instructions about how to draw
the shape of the skeleton's rib cage.

Child   It's a square

The teacher draws a VERY SMALL square.

Child   No, it's bigger

Teacher erases the first square and draws another which is TOO
BIG.

Child   No...It's sort of in between...

Eventually the children decide that it is not a perfect square, and
that the corners of the shape are rounded.

Quite often the teacher has to insist on moving on as the children can become quite obsessive about small differences! When this happens the teacher always stresses that the children will be able to include the details they are pointing out in their own drawings.

The teacher starts to use analogy when the class focus on the complicated pattern of ribs printed on the surface of the inflated 'chest'.

Teacher   Do those shapes remind you of anything?...Yes I see
                 what you mean... Look, it is a bit like curving branches
                 on a tree...[pointing to a rib curving away from the
                 breast bone] Can you hold your fingers up and make
                 that shape in the air?... Can you *count* the curves for me
                 so that I know how many to draw?

Physically demonstrating a shape can be helpful with individual children who have difficulty finding verbal language or are bilingual learners, allowing the teacher to feed in vocabulary in response to their actions. Asking the whole class to make a shape in this way can also be a useful strategy for involving every child, particularly in situations where more vocal members of the group are in danger of dominating the proceedings!

Once the curved ribs have been added to the drawing on the board, the teacher judges that it is time to bring the negotiated drawing exercise to a close.

The object of the exercise is to create a route towards the children's own drawings, so it is unnecessary to complete the drawing on the board. Stop the exercise well before the children begin to get bored so they will enjoy working in this way again!

❷ Developing the Context

The teacher now repositions the skeleton so that it is sitting on a chair in the middle of the room, and begins to build a story...

Teacher   One day when the children came in from play they heard a strange sobbing sound...They looked round to find out who was making this sad noise ... and saw a skeleton sitting on a chair crying!

The teacher gets one of the children to ask the skeleton why it is so unhappy. They learn that the skeleton used to be a dancing skeleton, but one day it woke up and found that it had forgotten how to dance! After a short discussion, the children decide that they will teach the skeleton how to dance. The teacher continues to narrate link sections of the story as the children get up, in turn, and show the skeleton some of the ways that they can dance. The skeleton gradually stops crying, and ends up thanking the children for their help as he dances out of the classroom.

The children have had a change in activity and a chance to 'stretch their legs'. There has been a lot of laughter in the classroom in the course of the story, and the skeleton has been placed in an imaginative 'frame' which the children can build on in their own pictures.

❸ The Children Make Their Own Drawings

When the active story making has come to a conclusion, the children return to their tables and the teacher's drawing is wiped off the board so that it cannot be 'copied'. The class are now invited to make their own drawings of the skeleton in the story, showing how it was taught to dance.

The skeleton is brought back into the centre of the room and arranged so that it is sitting on the chair again in full view of the class. The children are asked to refer to this 'real object' as they set about making their drawings of the dancing skeleton story. If they want to show the skeleton 'dancing' in their drawing, the children are able to go and change the position of its arms and legs to help them make their picture. The teacher provides individual help and encouragement where necessary.

The teacher–child interactions in the course of this session combine a range of different kinds of signals: verbal, visual and gestural. Judgements that the children are asked to make become progressively more difficult, and they have opportunities to practise precision in their instructions, using the kind of spatial language seldom required in general conversation. The children can learn from each other's use of language and the teacher brings into play differentiation through the level of demand made of individual children in the questioning process. The children enjoy the element of humour that runs through the lesson – it is fun to 'correct' your teacher!

● **2.2**

'Teaching the Skeleton How to Dance' – All these drawings were produced by children in Year 1.

A

In both **A** and **B** the children have indicated movement by changing the position of the limbs of the skeleton.

In drawing **B** the child has included a drawing of the teacher to the right of the picture depicting his glasses and moustache.

The child who made drawing **C** was initially reluctant to start and needed encouragement from the teacher who talked through the different parts of the skeleton with the child and a possible order in which they might be drawn. Following this individual attention, as you can see, an attempt was made to represent the shape of the pelvis and ribcage and to indicate the curving shape of each rib.

In both **A** and **D** the children have shown the overlap of the ribs and, in the latter drawing, the child has included the dark background printed on the model to indicate depth.

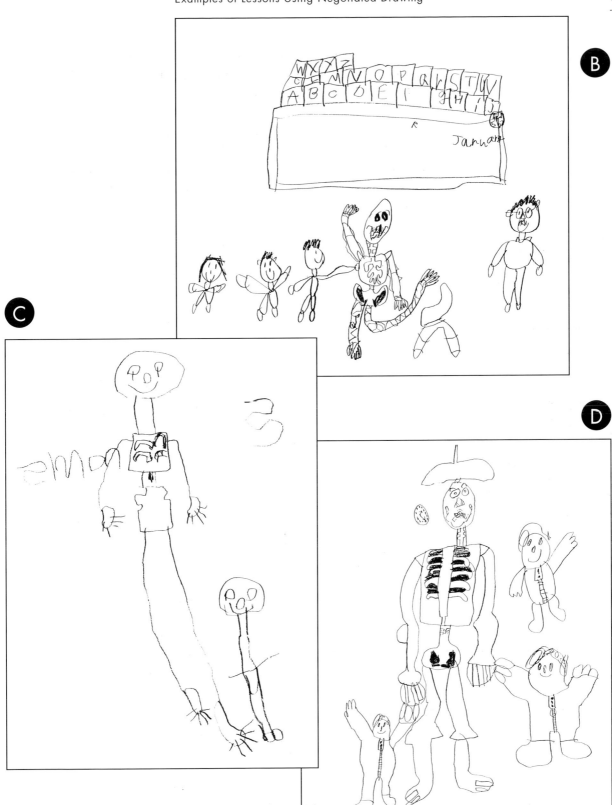

'By the time they come to school, all normal children can show skill as thinkers and language users to a degree which must compel our respect, so long as they are dealing with 'real-life' meaningful situations in which they have purposes and intentions and in which they recognise and respond to similar purposes and intentions in others.' (Donaldson, 1978)

The following two 'how to do it' drawing lessons are designed to use and build on the 'vernacular' knowledge that children bring with them to school. They provide opportunities for the children to share what they know from having observed adults at home, and rich opportunities for language work as they become 'teachers' themselves and have to translate this knowledge into readily understood instructions for someone else to follow. In other words, they are placed in an imaginative situation which is *meaningful* and provides motivation for their verbal language development, in addition to their development as 'artists' who are using the process of drawing as a mode of visual communication.

How to Fry an Egg!

This lesson has been used in a variety of different contexts, one being with a class of children in Year 1 who were engaged in the process of making a Cookery Book. After the negotiated drawing exercise, the teacher assumes the role of 'a person who does not know how to fry an egg', with the children being called upon to function as 'teachers'. This device of reversing the usual relationship between children and teacher is fun and provides opportunities for language development, which are emphasized in the commentary.

Real Objects
- portable electric cooker
- cooking oil
- box of eggs
- frying pan
- spatula
- knife
- fork
- plate

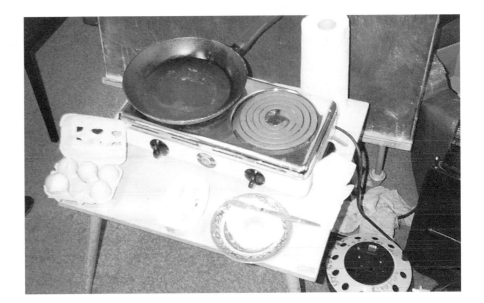

 Negotiated Drawing

The teacher brings a small electric cooker into the classroom and places it in front of the board. It is tilted in a position that enables all the children to have a good view of the top of the cooker with its two elements and the front surface on which the control knobs are located. The teacher ensures that there are no children sitting so far from the centre of the room that they gain a side perspective on this object.

First of all, members of the class are invited to make comparisons between this small cooker and the one in their own kitchen at home.

Links are made between this particular object and similar ones within the children's experience encouraging them to find language for describing the differences. This initial discussion touches on differences in design that are to do with the kind of energy used for cooking and involves the children in detailed descriptions of gas and electric cookers, microwave ovens, calor gas equipment, etc.

Teacher and class look closely at the cooker in the classroom and the function of the various parts of this piece of equipment.

The teacher is already beginning to 'focus' the way that the children look at the object by placing emphasis on SHAPE, and the RELATIONSHIP between different parts of the whole.

The children agree to help the teacher to make a drawing of the cooker on the board.

Teacher	Which part of the cooker should I draw first?
Child	The top...
Teacher	What shape is the top?
Children	...Square...

Although this is an obviously inaccurate description of the shape, the teacher proceeds to draw a big square on the board so that the children *themselves* will have the opportunity to draw attention to this!

The first conscious mistake the teacher makes in negotiating a drawing is important because it signals a lot to the children:
- *you have to think carefully about the PRECISE meaning of different words to do with shape;*
- *there is a 'game' element to this exercise because the teacher is following every instruction EXACTLY;*
- *instructions will need to be accurate and specific.*

Children	No!...Oblong!
	It's a rectangle!

The teacher erases the square and draws an oblong in its place. One of the children in the group keeps saying, 'It should be thinner!'. After careful questioning it becomes apparent that she is referring to the *front* of the cooker rather than the top. The teacher, therefore, adds another narrower rectangle positioned to represent the front of the cooker.

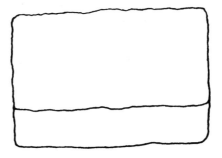

Children   Put the knobs on now...

The teacher draws two round 'switches' in the centre of the cooker, even though they are, in reality, positioned on either side of the front section!

Teacher	Is that where they should be?
Child	One there... and one there...[pointing towards the blackboard]
Teacher	When you say 'one there, and one there', what *exactly* do you mean? They're in the middle at the moment. Do you think that's wrong?
Child	She means one at one end...
Teacher	One at each end? I see...one towards this end on the right,...and one towards the other end on the left.

The teacher now corrects the drawing, and the interaction, which the children are obviously enjoying, continues.

Language development is being encouraged both in terms of spatial awareness and the relationship between different sections of a whole. The teacher uses humour to guard against this interaction becoming tedious! Although the children are being encouraged to find more appropriate language, the teacher ensures that nothing offered by an individual member of the class is received in a way which undermines confidence or makes the child feel stupid. This exercise is ideal for reinforcing language associated with maths.

Further instructions are given by the children.

Child	You have to put the two lines down the middle...
Teacher	You mean the bit your fingers hold [referring to the grips on the cooker switches]? Like that?
Child	Yes ... and the numbers...
Teacher	Do you mind if I leave the numbers out? It's just that the chalk is too thick ...You could put the numbers in your own drawings...

*The teacher explains **why** it seems inappropriate to try to put the numbers on the drawing on the board, but points out that this kind of detail is possible when you are using a pencil. This avoids the teacher getting involved in unnecessary detail, but also points a need to match particular tools to different drawing tasks.*

When attention is focused on the electric elements, the children, who have recently been looking closely at shells, explain that they are SPIRALS. These shapes are then added to the drawing on the board.

This interactive drawing process offers many opportunities for forming valuable links between different experiences and between different subject areas of the curriculum. Words begin to make a different kind of sense once they are applied in new contexts!

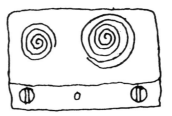

❷ Developing the Context

Once the drawing on the blackboard is complete, the teacher plugs in the electric cooker and, to the delight of the children, produces the frying pan, spatula, cooking oil and box of eggs!

At this point in the lesson it becomes apparent that the teacher is entering into 'pretend'. She explains to the class that she really wants to fry an egg but has no idea how to set about it. She 'wonders' if there is anyone in the room who might be able to help her by explaining exactly what she has to do..... There is a buzz of excitement as various children say they could help because they know what to do!

The children are being provided with an opportunity to use what they know from having observed a parent in the kitchen. They are also being asked to function as 'teachers' and realize that the 'game' element, apparent in the negotiated drawing exercise, still applies!

Teacher   What do I do next?
Child   Break the egg on the edge.
[The teacher mimes breaking the egg on the side of the TABLE!]
Child   No! You must break it on the edge of the pan...
Child   Put it in the pan...
Teacher   All of it?
Children   ...No... only the insides...

By pretending to know nothing about these procedures the teacher is able to elicit greater precision in the instructions from the children. The idea of an adult who does not know how to fry an egg is greatly enjoyed by the infants.

As the lesson proceeds, the children help the teacher to decide when the egg is cooked and how to transfer it from pan to plate without breaking the yolk. The teacher uses and then builds on the vocabulary employed by the children, reinforcing meanings and extending understandings as new words with more particular meanings are introduced into the discussion.

The teacher seems to enjoy a different kind of attention from the children when she is 'pretending', and there is a sense of fun in the classroom. However, a careful balance needs to be maintained between fuelling laughter by finding the most inappropriate ways of interpreting imprecise instructions and getting the children to really concentrate!

❸ The Children Make Their Own Drawings

In the final stage of the lesson the teacher asks the children to make a drawing of someone frying an egg. They are encouraged to make it the kind of picture which 'shows exactly what you have to do'.

The children are not being asked to make a 'fantasy' picture but one that conveys information about a practical activity – they are still functioning as 'teachers'.

The teacher explains that the figure in their drawing could be the person they have just watched frying an egg, or it might be themselves in their kitchen at home. (This group of children had drawn their own kitchen from memory the previous week.) At this point the teacher's drawing is wiped off the board to avoid it being used as a model.

The process in which the children are engaged never involves 'copying'. The teacher's drawing has served its purpose as a means of introducing the children to a process of careful looking and mark making, and it is important that it is no longer used as a reference point.

The cooker, which has now cooled down, is placed in a prominent position in the classroom. The teacher suggests that the children should come up and look at it closely if they need to in the course of making their pictures.

As the children engage in drawing, the teacher moves about the room settling those who are slow to begin, and helping individuals with their pictures through discussion.

The teacher has assumed her normal role once more!

As children finish their drawings they discuss them with their teacher and those who are still interested in frying eggs are encouraged to write out a sequence of instructions which can be placed in relation to their picture.

They are starting to make a real Cookery Book!

In **A** and **B** the children have included numbering to help the viewer read the sequence of actions involved in frying an egg.

On the right of the picture in drawing **A**, the child is explaining what has to be done to a visitor from another planet whose spacecraft hovers overhead. (See the imaginative context developed using drama in the next lesson 'How to Make a Sandwich'.)

● **2.3**
'How to Fry an Egg' – A,B,C and D were produced by children in Year 1, and E and F are by children in Year 2

Note the different ways in which the children have depicted the table legs. In some of these pictures we see an aerial view of the cooker; sometimes, as in **D**, the top and front surface seem to have been unfolded so as to lie flat on the table. Note the side views drawn in **C** and how these contrast with the 'splayed out' views in **D**.

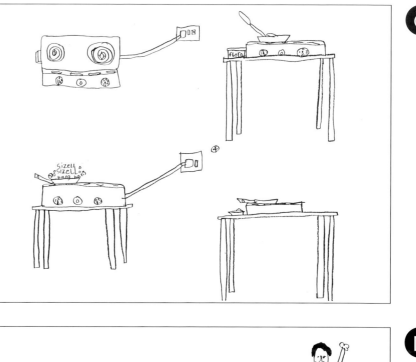

C

D

In drawing **E** the older child has added annotation to her illustration for the Cookery Book. The child who made drawing **F** is at a less advanced stage of development but all the essential elements are present – the cooker which is plugged into a wall socket, the table laid for a meal and the cook holding a frying pan as two figures watch the meal being prepared.

How to Make a Sandwich

In this lesson the teacher uses DRAMA, adopting the role of 'a stranger from another planet' to create a context which will stretch the children's thinking. It has been used successfully as part of a sequence of drawing lessons with both Year 1 classes and children towards the end of their year in a Reception class. Commentary in this account of the lesson emphasizes the 'teacher thinking', which underpins use of drama to create a context for the children's drawings.

Real Objects

- bread knife
- table knife
- spoon
- margarine
- whole loaf of bread
- breadboard
- jar of marmite
- peanut butter

 Negotiated Drawing

The teacher shows the children all the ingredients and equipment that have been brought into the classroom – the real objects. She asks them if they can suggest what you could make with these things.

The teacher is starting both to assess and tap what the children know from having observed adults preparing food. (Teachers working with an older group of children might well want to omit this initial discussion so that a question of this kind could be posed later in the lesson when the teacher is in role.)

Teacher and children discuss the difference between the two knives – one designed for 'cutting' and the other suitable for 'spreading'.

Before the negotiated drawing begins, the teacher is engaging the children in careful looking and exploring relationships between the design of tools and their function.

The children are now asked to help their teacher to draw the bread knife on the blackboard. In the course of this negotiated drawing exercise, deliberate mistakes are made by the teacher and then rubbed out as they are pointed out by the children.

With a relatively simple shape, like that of the knife selected for this exercise, the 'mistakes' made by the teacher tend to be to do with scale, such as the size of the handle in relation to the blade of the knife.

Members of the class suggest how the teacher's drawing needs to be amended in order to arrive at a more accurate representation of the bread knife.

When the negotiated drawing of the knife has been completed, the teacher clears a space in the classroom in preparation for the drama.

❷ Developing the Context

The teacher explains to the class that in a minute they are all going to start a drama. She is going to pretend to be someone else, a very special visitor who comes to their classroom one day.

Teacher   In a moment I am going to walk over to the door, and when I turn round I am going to be someone from another planet... Watch and listen very carefully, and let's see what you can find out about this visitor...

*First of all the teacher makes sure that all the children understand that they are going to be involved in a 'make-believe'. If she is worried that the children's perception of 'someone from another planet' is 'little green monster which makes strange noises' she might narrate how the special visitor from space finds its way to their classroom. This would allow the teacher to include detail about how 'the stranger **looks** very like an Earth person but is wearing a shiny silver space suit...'*

The teacher walks to the side of the room, and pauses to ensure that the full attention of the class is focused on what is about to happen before turning round. She then slowly turns to face the class looking a little apprehensive...

*The teacher avoids adopting behaviour which is too exaggerated, but signals clearly that the visitor is rather nervous. This provides a contrast between the fictitious role she has adopted and her normal attitude towards the children. By making the visitor someone who has to be 'put at ease' she is placing responsibility on the pupils – **they** will have to take charge! A ploy of this kind means that the children will have to think carefully about all that they say and do as they begin to interact with the role.*

At first there are a few giggles as the children come to terms with the new situation, but the teacher in role remains 'completely serious' and waits for the children to find appropriate ways of responding.

By patiently staying in role, the teacher is giving the children the time they need to adapt to the new situation. Her seriousness signals to the class that this is a drama that everyone needs to take seriously. The children are all aware of the fact that they are entering into 'make-believe' and the giggles are to do with enjoying this idea even though they may be a little self-conscious at the start.

The teacher in role asks the children if it is all right to come into their classroom and then introduces herself as a visitor from another planet. The children greet the stranger and begin to introduce themselves, explaining that they are all members of Ms X's class! As this dialogue develops they find themselves having to explain what being 'at school' means and why they are there.

The role the teacher has adopted is being used to get the children to step back from, and consider, all the things which they take for granted in their normal daily lives. Their explanation includes interesting description, and comments about their normal relationship with the teacher they are at present interacting with in role! Although much of what the children have to say is extremely amusing, their teacher remains in role as the visitor from another planet, taking all that the children say seriously.

The teacher is aware that sufficient time has been spent on establishing the fictitious context and begins to move the drama on. She explains, in role as the visitor, that a museum is being constructed on her home planet which is going to include a section on Earth people's food. She is particularly interested in an exhibit about 'How to Make Sandwiches' and wants to know if they can teach her about this process.

*A situation has been created in which it is the **children** who have the expertise and will have to find ways of explaining what they know to an adult – a reversal of normal classroom dynamics. This strategy, which was developed by the Drama in Education pioneer Dorothy Heathcote, is described in drama terms as giving the children the 'mantle of the expert'.*

The visitor is taught by the children how to use the utensils which have been placed on a table, and learns how to cut and butter bread for sandwiches. The filling for the sandwiches is selected, and the visitor learns about the need for 'cling film' or 'lunch boxes' if food like this is to be kept until it is dinner time. The visitor poses questions about points she does not understand, and in this way the teacher is able to stretch the children and provide positive reinforcement when they are struggling to explain.

Throughout the development of this session all the children are engaged and enjoy 'playing out the fiction' and interacting with their teacher in a new way. The teacher is able to remain in role throughout this section of the work but she is aware of the fact that she can stop the drama at any time and speak to the children as their teacher if this becomes necessary. It is important to realize that children have no difficulty in slipping in and out of drama as long as the teacher's signals are clear. (In their own make-believe play they are constantly stopping the 'pretend', to sort out what they are going to do next and then entering the make-believe again.)

The drama concludes with the teacher in role trying to remember all that the children have taught her, and asking the class if they could possibly make some drawings of 'How to Make a Sandwich' for display in the Space Museum.

The drama is being used to motivate the drawing task which will follow, giving the children a sense of 'audience' for their work.

The teacher brings the drama to a close before there is any loss in concentration. She thanks them for all their help, and says how much she is looking forward to seeing their drawings before she says goodbye.

It is important to try to stop the drama when the children are all still fully engaged. The drama can always be picked up again on a later occasion, with the teacher really exploiting the role she has adopted to create new learning opportunities for the children. There might be all sorts of other 'exhibits' that the children could provide for the Space Museum relating to work in other curriculum areas, or the class could go on to develop a drama about going on a voyage to another planet!

Before bringing the lesson to a close there is some important discussion out of role. The teacher asks the children about what they discovered about the visitor from another planet and how they felt when participating in the drama. They are obviously interested in the idea of the Space Museum and the teacher decides that she will exploit it by making a special display of the drawings that the children produce.

Reflective discussion out of role is a crucial element of the drama process. Children gain from making comparisons between what they say and do in the 'make-believe' and what they understand and believe in reality. This kind of discussion deepens their understanding of drama as an art form, allowing them to assume greater responsibility for the shaping of future work. It also provides the teacher with important feedback, which will help her to structure future learning opportunities using drama.

❸ The Children Make Their Own Drawings

When the children return from break, the teacher's drawing has been erased from the board. The children now sit at their normal tables and the teacher focuses them into the drawing task, linking this to the 'How to Make a Sandwich' display for the Space Museum. She emphasizes that their drawings will need to be nice and clear because they are for people who have never made a sandwich before.

Members of the class are presented with the option of showing how to make a sandwich in one drawing or producing a sequence of smaller drawings showing each stage of the process. The real objects, which have been used in the course of the session, are on display for the children to refer to in the course of this work.

Individual children are given support where necessary as the teacher moves round the room looking at the children's work and encouraging them to tell her about the detail of their drawings.

Note the range of drawings produced by children in the same Reception class. **A** and **B** are two sophisticated sequential drawings

● **2.4**
'How to Make a Sandwich' –
A,B,C and D are by children
in a Reception class, and E
and F were produced by
children in Year 1

which show an ability to communicate the **process** of sandwich making. Only the top half of the sandwich-maker is visible, behind the table from our point of view.

Drawing **C** was produced by a bilingual learner and in the course of the lesson common visual reference points provided an ideal focus for developing verbal language. This child has also indicated sequence in the drawing.

The 4-year-old child responsible for drawing **D**, although at a less advanced stage of development than some of the others, clearly depicts a difference between the two knives and shows where the loaf has been cut.

The older boy who produced drawing **E** is obviously interested in visual details like the texture of the bread and decoration on the clothing of the sandwich-maker. Another boy in the class who produced drawing **F** has made an accurate depiction of the knife but used a more diagrammatic form of representation for the sandwich-making process. On the right of his picture he includes both the visitor from another planet and the sandwich-maker tasting the end product.

Capturing a Dinosaur

A lesson in which the children travel back in time to capture a dinosaur without hurting it! This was originally devised for children in Year 2 who were doing a class project on Prehistoric Creatures, but has also been successfully used with children in Year 1.

Real Objects

A selection of brightly coloured plastic dinosaurs (The models chosen for this lesson comprised three different creatures, approximately 16 x 40 centimetres – large enough for the whole class to focus on just **one** of these models for the negotiated drawing exercise.)

Negotiated Drawing

The teacher selects one of the large plastic models – 'stegosaurus' – and shows it to the class, asking if anyone knows what it is called. A discussion follows in which members of the class share what they know about dinosaurs.

*The starting point is always the knowledge that the children bring to the lesson and what they can see in front of them, rather than the teacher **telling** the class about the real object.*

The teacher now places the model in front of the drawing board in a position in which the whole class can see the creature.

The teacher knows that the children are interested in the two ridges of 'lozenge' shapes above the stegosaurus' spine and may want to draw these first. However, this will not be a good starting point for the negotiated drawing because of difficulties to do with coordinating these shapes in relation to each other. In this instance the children are not asked to suggest how to begin the drawing but, instead, are asked by the teacher to help him to draw the curving back of the creature.

When the children are asked to describe the shape of the creature's back, they compare it to a rising 'hill'. The teacher draws this suggestion but deliberately exaggerates the curve of the line on the board.

The children complain that this curve is 'much too big' or 'too high'. They are then asked to imagine that they are starting from the creature's nose and to make the shape of its back in the air with their forefinger so that he can see what they mean. When this is done, the teacher says he sees what they mean, the curve is too steep. He then rectifies the shape on the board.

Making shapes in the air can be a useful way of getting children who are less articulate to demonstrate what they mean, enabling the teacher to then feed in appropriate vocabulary for describing the shape. (Sometimes it can be helpful to ask just one child to come to the front of the class and 'demonstrate' for all to see.)

Now that there is a line on the board in relation to which other shapes can be placed, the children start to try to describe the shapes on the spinal ridge, which they are obviously keen for the teacher to draw. There is a lot of discussion about what to call these shapes including suggestions like 'triangles on top of rectangles'.

The teacher asks the children if all the shapes on the creature's back are the same and the children point out that those towards the centre are far 'bigger' and 'taller' than the ones towards the end of the row.

The dialogue that develops focuses on shape, scale and making comparisons. There is obviously potential for making direct connections between this kind of drawing exercise and work in maths. Negotiated drawing is a much richer process when it is contextualized within the whole curriculum.

Discussion follows about whether the creature is looking 'upwards' or 'downwards' and the consequent position of the head in relation to the rest of the body. Comparisons are also made between the creature's hind legs and smaller forelegs, with the children being asked to surmise about possible reasons for this difference in size.

The teacher brings the negotiated drawing exercise to a close without including the creature's head and legs in his drawing on the board. He tells the children that they will have a chance to draw the complete creature in their own pictures.

It is often a disadvantage for the teacher to complete an image when working in this way. An incomplete drawing on the board means that each child will have to make his or her own assessments of shape at the start of their personal drawings. It also avoids children becoming inhibited because they feel they don't have sufficient skills to match the adult's drawing. It's not an exercise to do with demonstrating how well the teacher draws!

❷ Developing the Context

The teacher now begins to set up a drama exercise for the children. Tables are pushed back so that there will be more room for the drama and the children find a space of their own and sit down.

The teacher tells the class that he knows how good they are at 'pretending' and asks them all to imagine that they have a time machine which will enable them all to travel back to the world in which the dinosaurs lived.

Teacher   A group of brave volunteers have been selected to go on a special scientific mission because of their courage and expertise... Their task is to try to capture a great prehistoric creature without hurting it, so that the people of today can learn more about dinosaurs and how they used to live ...

Narration is used to progress this fantasy to a point at which the children have been transported back to prehistoric times and are hiding, watching giant reptiles in their natural habitat.

A fictitious context has been established, and now the class are ready to move into practical drama activities. (This lesson did in actual fact precede the film 'Jurassic Park'!)

Either individually or with a friend the children begin to act out their own drama. The teacher remains at the edge of the room, facilitating the drama by freezing the action from time to time and building in tension through further narration. Sometimes individual children are asked to voice what they can 'hear' or 'see' in the world to which they have been transported. Time is provided for all to accomplish their task, with the children miming the building of traps and the capture of their creature.

The drama is brought to a conclusion when all have checked that the prehistoric creature which they have caught has not been harmed in any way and they are ready to return to the present so that it can be thoroughly examined.

An imaginative context has now been created which has fuelled the children's interest in dinosaurs. They have had a change in activity and will now be ready to sit still and concentrate on drawing. They also have had an 'adventure' which they will be able to re-live and elaborate in the course of their picture making.

The teacher does not ask the children to share verbal accounts of their adventure at this point in time. What each child experienced in the drama will be channelled into the drawing exercise.

❸ The Children Make Their Own Drawings

The children return to their tables and the teacher wipes his own drawing from the blackboard. Model dinosaurs are placed on each table so that every child has the opportunity to look closely at a model in the course of constructing a picture of their adventure.

Although the children may have had a partner to work with in the drama activity, each child makes his or her own individual drawing of 'how to capture a dinosaur without hurting it'.

In many cases the model which has been placed on the children's table is different from the one that the teacher selected to draw. The children are therefore being placed in a situation in which they need to bring into play for themselves the 'careful looking', 'questioning' and 'decision-making' process that they earlier engaged in as a whole class. The negotiated drawing has merely provided them with a guide for finding their own ways forward.

As the children start to draw, the teacher moves round from table to table knowing that a few children will need some additional help. Two different kinds of questions are posed to support them in the picture-making process. 'Observation' is the focus when discussing the children's representation of the dinosaur, with the teacher posing questions about the *shapes* the child can see and the *surface texture* of the model. When the imaginative aspects of the picture are being discussed the questions are about the detail of the child's experience in the drama – 'How exactly did you *do* that?', followed by 'How could you *show* that in your drawing?'

Most of the children are able to work without the help of the teacher. This is not the first lesson in their drawing programme, and the skills focused upon in the negotiated drawing have become part of their own personal repertoire.

As children finish their drawings they have an opportunity to tell their teacher and friends about their adventure, referring to their pictures as they speak about the detail of all that happened to them in their imagined experience. They have obviously enjoyed the lesson and their storytelling is rich and full of vivid images.

The children have been engaged in drawing from observation, but they have used the real object as a reference point or aid to extend their imaginative picture making – a process is used by adult artists. The fact that each child could base his or her drawing on something which had already been allowed to grow in the imagination created an easy starting point for the picture.

Drawings **A, B** and **C** were made by children who were working from a model identical to the one used for the negotiated drawing exercise. Drawing **D**, based on a different model dinosaur, illustrates how easily children can transfer looking and recording skills to a new object. Notice how all the children have started to record the surface texture of the models.

● **2.5**

'How to Capture a Dinosaur Without Hurting It' – Drawings A, B, C, D and E were produced by children in Year 1 and F by a child in Year 2

In drawing **F** you can see how the pit which was dug to trap the dinosaur has been carefully lined with soft vegetation to prevent the creature from getting hurt. The child has obviously enjoyed using texture to represent this. You can also see the net designed to prevent the dinosaur from escaping stretched over the pit and attached by ropes to the trunks of surrounding trees.

The 'adventure' element of the drama has been captured in all these drawings and details of the elaborate schemes which the children developed for trapping the dinosaurs without hurting them. **This type of richness is very characteristic of pictures made by children after they have participated in 'experiential' forms of drama.**

Things to Remember

What Materials Do the Children Need?

Pencils

For the kind of work described in this book it is important that the children use **standard size pencils which have a soft, dark lead – B, 2B or 3B.**

Larger pencils and crayons frustrate attempts to define detail, and it is useful to limit children to working without colour as a contrast to other aspects of the art curriculum. Using normal size pencils has the further advantage of providing an opportunity for the children to exercise the fine motor skills required for writing.

Erasers

The children should have access to erasers when drawing so that, like their teacher, they can **re-consider and re-draft their images.** On other occasions, children will be encouraged to make big, bold marks in their art work, but in this situation they are engaged in a process of carefully considered mark making.

Paper

Any paper on which a pencil line shows up clearly can be used for this kind of drawing, but try to avoid paper which tears easily as the children will be using erasers.

All the original children's drawings provided as illustrations in this book were done on **A3 copy paper, which is easily obtainable and not too expensive.** Children enjoy this larger size paper, and their ideas and drawings soon expand to fill the extra space.

Try to get paper larger than A4, although using paper of this size may create difficulties to do with finding enough space for the children to work in. However, using smaller paper is better than not drawing at all!

Some "Do"s and "Don't"s

Rulers

There are some children who will automatically reach for rulers or objects that they can draw round to make precise shapes in their pictures. In an exercise of this kind which is geared towards developing and refining drawing skills it is sensible to discourage children from using this type of aid.

Felt Tipped Pens

Many children are used to drawing with felt tips, but allowing them to use these in work of this kind cuts out opportunities for learning from the marks they make which don't seem 'right'. Using a pencil means that the children can make a sequence of amendments, erasing 'mistakes' until they are happy with the outcome of their drawing.

Teacher Questioning

Teachers need to think carefully about what they say to children when they are engaged in the drawing process. Carefully posed questions about shapes that can be defined in the real object, or the shapes which the child has made on paper, **enable children to correct their own misjudgements**. This is far more effective than being **told** by teacher!

Offering Praise

Above all else the children need to be encouraged and given lots of positive reinforcement so that they begin to develop **confidence** in their own drawing ability.

The need for careful looking, as well as encouraging the children to refer back to the model or real object, when they are making their own pictures has been stressed. However, it is also important to remember that the children are not just drawing from observation. They are using this representational image in a more imaginative frame and, therefore, may be including other exploratory drawing and possibly other conventions that they feel are appropriate. For example, a child may draw some lines behind his own drawing of a dinosaur to suggest that, in the story they have invented, the creature was moving really fast and was very difficult to catch! In reality these lines cannot be seen, but the child is using a perfectly acceptable convention for showing movement and this is an aspect of the drawing which needs to be acknowledged by the teacher in a positive way.

Exhibiting Work

Making displays of the children's drawings, and including the real object that provided the stimulus makes an interesting exhibition for the public spaces within the school.

Check List of Reminders!

✔ Choose large objects to draw which have clear shapes and are not too complicated.

✔ Avoid placing objects so that there are parts projecting forward so you don't have problems to do with 'foreshortening'.

✔ Seat the children so that they can all see the object you are going to draw from a **similar point of view**.

✔ Position the board so that all the class can see your drawing, and you can move to look at the object **from a similar perspective to the children**.

✔ Don't obstruct their view with your own body!

✔ Make it clear that it is the **children's** responsibility to guide the teacher!

✔ Make **deliberate mistakes** in your drawing when the children's instructions are not clear enough.

✔ Exploit the process of negotiated drawing for **language development** by progressively demanding more precise language and clearer instructions.

✔ Don't forget how helpful **analogy** can be when you are trying to describe shapes.

✔ Bilingual learners and less articulate children can participate by being asked to make shapes in the air with their fingers.

✔ Make as many **connections** as possible with work in other curriculum areas like maths and science.

✔ It's better not to complete the drawing on the board – stop once the exercise has served its purpose.

✔ Plan a way of contextualizing the object the children will draw in a way that is exciting or funny, so that the drawing task which you set is as interesting as possible.

✔ Once the children are familiar with this way of working 'drawing from observation' can become the context!

✔ Rub out your own drawing before the children begin theirs.

✔ Encourage the children to go and look at the real object when they are doing their own drawings.

✔ Support the **imaginative** aspects of the children's drawings as well as their observational drawing.

✔ Provide opportunities for the children to **talk about their drawings and explain the detail of all that is happening in their pictures.** If the teacher cannot give this kind of individual attention to each child it can be very productive to **get the children to talk about their pictures in pairs.**

More Ideas for Lessons

This section of the book contains a selection of brief outlines of other lessons and reproductions of some of the children's drawings generated by the lessons.

Negotiated drawing is a feature of most of these lessons but, in some cases, the lessons were designed for children who were already sufficiently experienced in this way of working to be able to embark on a drawing from observation without a great deal of preparatory support. You will also see that in other instances it was not appropriate for the teacher to develop an imaginative context for the work as the children had reached a stage at which they were sufficiently well motivated and confident to undertake a drawing from observation without this. Just drawing directly from first-hand experience is enjoyable for the children once they have developed confidence in their skills.

The Magic Bicycle

Real Object

A bicycle

❶ Negotiated Drawing

Following discussion about the function of various parts of the bicycle, the teacher asks the class to help her to draw a wheel and part of the frame.

❷ Developing the Context

Before completing the negotiated drawing, the teacher secretes an envelope somewhere on the bicycle where the children will notice it before long! When the children point it out she holds it up and asks for a volunteer to open it. Inside there is a note which says 'I AM A MAGIC BICYCLE, AND I CAN HELP YOU!' The class then share their ideas about the different ways in which a bicycle could be magic, inventing their own stories.

❸ The Children Make Their Own Drawings

Each child draws his or her own 'magic bicycle' story, referring to the real object which is left in a prominent position in the classroom.

● **4.1**
'The Magic Bicycle' – All these drawings were produced by children in Year 1

Drawings **A** and **B** show a real balance between observation of a bicycle and the imaginative context that the children have developed.

In drawing **A** the magic bicycle has transported its rider to sea, with pirates in their elaborate ship on the left of the picture.
In drawing **B** we are provided with a depiction of the landscape through which the bicycle has been ridden before reaching the coast.

The child who produced drawing **C** has transformed the bicycle into a 'BMX' and the boy responsible for drawing **D** has, of his own accord, drawn a rear (on the right) as well as side (on the left) elevation of the bicycle.

Hanging Out the Washing

Real Objects
A washing line stretched across the classroom with large and small articles of clothing pegged along it

Negotiated Drawing

The children discuss the clothes on the line, with the teacher focusing on **scale** and the **patterns** on the garments. The teacher then selects one item of clothing, pegging it so that all the children can see this clearly in relation to the board on which she is going to draw.

❷ Developing the Context

There is lots of discussion about getting dirty and washing and drying clothes before the children are invited to **find their own context** for the washing line.

❸ The Children Make Their Own Drawings

Members of the class decide whether the washing in their drawing is going to be a picture of what happens 'at home', or a washing line in a story they have invented. As each picture is completed, the children have a chance to tell their teacher about the detail of the context they have chosen. Every child has paid attention to the patterns on the garments in these drawings and there is a clear indication of observed differences in scale between items of clothing.

In drawings **A**, **B** and **D** the children have captured the curve of the washing line in their pictures. Note the detailed attention given to the pegs in drawing **A**.

In drawing **B** the child has managed to show the tilt of the head in the rear view of the figure reaching up to the line in the centre of the picture, and has included both a front and side view of other figures.

● **4.2**
'Hanging Out the Washing' –
All these drawings were
produced by children in
Year 1

Picture **C** conveys the impression of a very jolly scene – a grinning sun with all its little attendant suns, as well as clouds with smiling faces. This child's drawing shows the influence of conventions used in illustrations in children's books and advertising, etc. which she enjoys and has incorporated into her own work.

Drawing **D** was made by a bilingual child from a Japanese background. Although the two figures are rather schematic, there is a lot of detail included in the clothes on the line and attention is paid to different shapes and sizes.

Creatures who Live in a Shoe

Real Objects
A collection of boots
and shoes

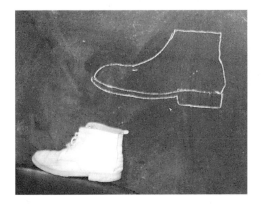

 Negotiated Drawing

The teacher selects a large walking boot and places it where
everyone can see it. The children discuss the design qualities of this
boot before they start to make a negotiated drawing with their
teacher on the board.

 Developing the Context

The teacher asks the class if they know any stories about animals or
small people who live in a boot, or might convert a shoe into a
home. These ideas are shared with the whole group.

3 The Children Make Their Own Drawings

The teacher asks the children to select a boot or shoe and place it in
front of them on their table. (Taking off one of their own shoes is an
easy way of providing real models for this exercise.) Now each child
uses this as a focus for observational drawing linked with their own
story about small creatures or people who convert a shoe into a
home.

In these drawings you can see a real interest in the detail of the
footwear used as a model. In each case the children have shown in

● **4.3**
'Creatures who Live in a Shoe'
– All these drawings were
produced by children in
Year 1

their drawings how the various occupants enter their 'home'. Note the stairway leading to the 'trainer' in **A**, the door in the heel of the 'walking shoe' in **B** and creatures entering their stylish 'boot' home in drawings **C** and **D**.

In drawing **B** there is a table laid for breakfast (bottom right) and a bird viewing the whole scene.

A

B

In **C** the mice are carrying cheese into their home while the cat (to the right) is trying to catch a bird.

The girl who made drawing **D** has included a 'life size' human figure and cat which emphasizes differences in scale. Note the detailed way in which the child has indicated how the boot is laced and the cat's paw touching the girl's hand.

Swimming in the Sea

(This lesson presents more difficult drawing problems for the children and was designed to be used towards the end of a sequence of drawing lessons.)

Real Objects

A human model (a child volunteer who is able to keep still), collection of plastic crabs and fish, pieces of seaweed

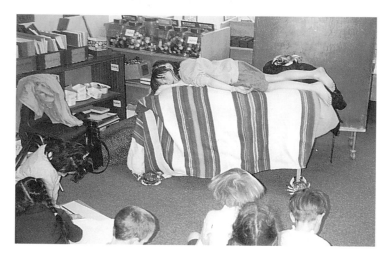

Negotiated Drawing

The teacher puts cushions on a low table in front of the blackboard. The child model lies prone on the cushions with arms supported in a 'swimming position', and the near arm placed in a way which does not obscure the head. The teacher then negotiates a drawing of part of this swimmer.

❷ Developing the Context

The children share experiences about swimming in the sea and discuss the sea creatures or objects which people might want to include when they make their own pictures of a swimmer. They also discuss whether they want their swimmer to be wearing everyday clothes like the model or would prefer to replace these with an imagined swimsuit.

❸ The Children Make Their Own Drawings

The children are encouraged to look carefully at the model, paying particular attention to the position of the limbs.

It is interesting to see the way that these children have attempted to show a three-quarter view of the swimmer's head which reflects their own view of the observed human model, and much attention has been paid to the detail of fingers and toes. All have chosen to replace the school uniform worn by the model with a patterned swimsuit.

In drawings **A**, **B** and **D** some reference has been made to the plastic fish and crabs which were placed around the classroom.

The child who made drawing **B** has elaborated the context to include dialogue with a predatory shark!

● **4.4**
'Swimming in the Sea' – All these drawings were produced by children in Year 1

Note how in drawing C the curve of the swimmer's hands and feet mirror the rhythm of the waves and give a real sense of movement through water.

The Fox and the Stork

Real Objects
- 'stuffed' stork
- an old fox fur
- plate
- tall glass vase

❶ Negotiated Drawing

The teacher places the stork where all can see it and begins a negotiated drawing of the large bird.

❷ Developing the Context

The teacher borrows from the Aesop's fable, *The Fox and the Stork*. 'A Fox invited a Stork to dinner one day intending to play a practical joke on his guest. He gave her some stew to eat but put it on a *flat* plate. Because the Stork had such a long thin beak she could not lap up the stew so the Fox greedily ate both dishes of food... The following day, the Stork invited the Fox to dinner to get her revenge. She made some stew and served it in a tall narrow vase so that the Fox was unable to get his head below the rim to eat...' As the teacher tells the story she uses the real objects she has brought into the classroom to demonstrate the appropriateness of the shape of the containers for each animal in the story.

❸ The Children Make Their Own Drawings

All the objects are placed where the children can refer to them as they begin to make their own drawings showing the practical joke played on the stork and how she got her revenge.

In each of these pictures, the 'stance' of the stork used as the model for the negotiated drawing has been changed by the children in order to illustrate what happened in the story.

In drawing **A** the stork is represented with a side view and the aerial view of the fox with its legs splayed mirrors the flatness of the fox fur used as a model.

The girl who made drawing **B** has indicated the movement of the stork as it tries to reach the food in the tall, narrow container.

● **4.5**
'The Fox and the Stork' – All these drawings were produced by children in Year 1

In drawing **C** all the animals are depicted with an aerial view.

The child who made drawing **D** appears to have developed a context within which the stork is suspended from an aeroplane as he attempts to reach down into the tall vase.

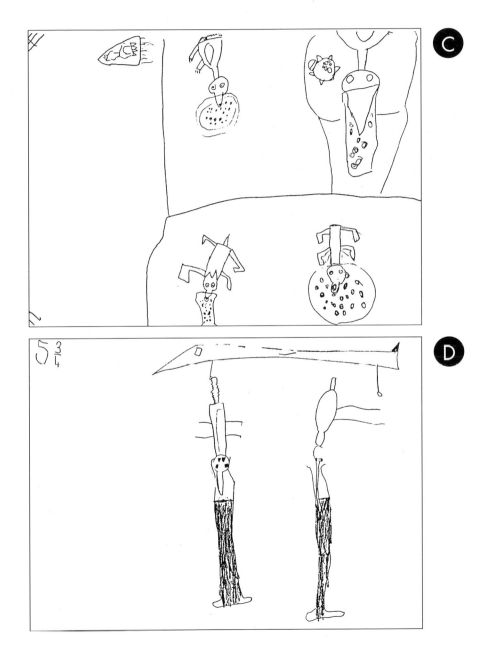

Weighing an Elephant

Real Object
An old-fashioned set of kitchen scales

Negotiated Drawing

After discussing the purpose of scales and how they are used, the teacher begins a negotiated drawing of the object on the board.

Developing the Context

The teacher creates a fictitious context for the children's drawings by adopting a role – an animal keeper with a problem! She explains that she has an enormous elephant which needs to be weighed. The children are divided into small groups and asked to make a mime of how they will lift the elephant onto the scales. Each group is then invited to show their mime to the rest of the class.

The Children Make Their Own Drawings

The children make their own pictures of weighing an elephant, imagining the elephant, but referring to the kitchen scales to help them with their pictures.

● **4.6**
'How to Weigh an Elephant' –
All these drawings were
produced by children in
Year 2

In drawing **A** the child has gone for a very carefully observed pair of scales, adding density to the image with shading; whereas in drawings **B**, **C** and **D** the children have obviously been more interested in drawing the humorous storyline.

In **B**, **C** and **D** occlusion has been used to show the tusk on the far side of the elephant's head. The boy who made drawing B has also used occlusion to place the heads of the two human figures in front of the elephant's body and their legs in front of the object on the floor as they heave the animal into the air. Note too the way that he has added texture to the elephant's skin.

In drawings **C** and **D** the children have borrowed the comic strip convention of 'speech bubbles' in order to provide a more detailed account of what is taking place in the frozen moment of narrative which they have depicted.

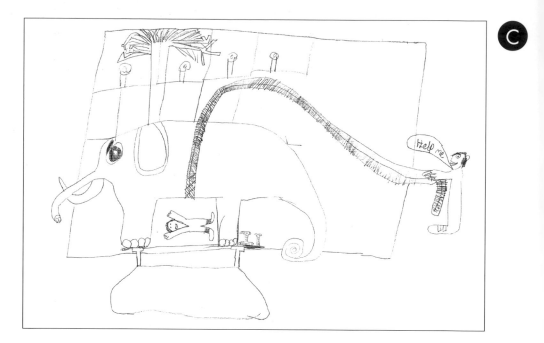

C

D

Mother and Child

Real Objects

A boy or girl volunteer, posing
with a life-size doll

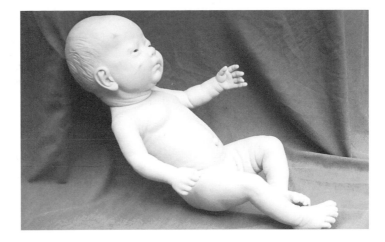

❶ Negotiated Drawing

The teacher asks children in the class to help the volunteer find the
best way to hold a young baby. When all are happy with the pose,
the teacher begins to make a negotiated drawing of the cradled doll.

❷ Developing the Context

(This lesson was designed for the period leading up to Christmas.)
The image of a mother and child is contextualized by the children
looking at and discussing reproductions of Mary Cassatt's and
Henry Moore's work on this theme, and postcard reproductions of
paintings of the Nativity from the National Gallery. (Keeping
appropriate Christmas cards is a cheap way of gathering resource
materials.)

❸ The Children Make Their Own Drawings

The children make their own Nativity pictures referring to both the
model holding the doll and, if they wish, the postcards of other
artists' work.

These drawings all show the influence of the seated model holding the baby used for the negotiated drawing, and the reproductions of work of other artists which the children looked at and talked about prior to starting their own pictures.

● **4.7**
'Christmas Drawings' – All these drawings were produced by children in Year 2

A Crocodile in the Classroom

Real Object

A large fabric crocodile

❶ Negotiated Drawing

The teacher places the crocodile where all the class can see it, and opens the jaw so that the children can discuss the teeth and the way that the jaw is hinged. The class then help the teacher to make a negotiated drawing of the crocodile.

❷ Developing the Context

The teacher begins to make up a story, 'One day, when their teacher was not looking, the classroom door was nudged open and an enormous crocodile crawled into the room...' The teacher then invites the children to suggest what happens next. The fabric crocodile is placed on the floor and individual children come and 'pose' key moments of their story with the large fabric crocodile.

❸ The Children Make Their Own Drawings

The children make their own drawings of adventures with the crocodile that visited their school. The fabric crocodile is left for the children to refer to in the course of their drawings, but the teacher's drawing is rubbed off the board.

Although the drawing programme outlined in this book was not designed for pre-school children, we were often invited to work with children in nurseries attached to local primary schools. The children who produced drawings **A**, **B** and **C** were approximately 3.5 years old.

● **4.8**
'A Crocodile in the Classroom' – A selection of drawings produced by children in a Nursery, a Reception class and Year 1

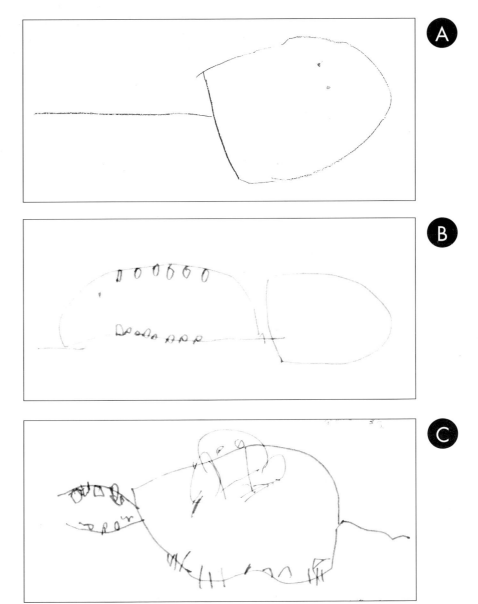

You can see that the child responsible for drawing **A** was able to differentiate between the head and body of the crocodile (with eyes) and its tail. In drawing **B,** the child has divided the creature into a head and tail and you can see the eye and teeth clearly marked on the head. In drawing **C**, the jaws are depicted as open – something a lot of Reception children find very difficult to do. The girl who made this picture has included herself going for a ride on the crocodile's back in the way that she had earlier physically 'demonstrated' to other children in the nursery. Note the series of three 'dashes' at the bottom of the crocodile that denote the creature's toes which the children had delighted in counting when they examined the fabric crocodile.

In drawings **D, E** and **F**, made by children who were 4 or just 5-years-old, there is evidence of further development. Look at the

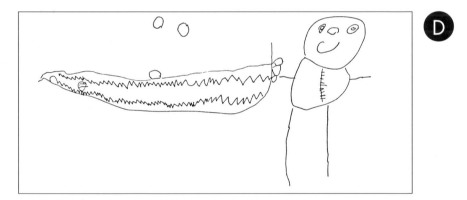

D

E

patterning on the crocodile in drawings **E** and **F**. In the former drawing you can see one child inside the jaws of the crocodile about to be saved by her friend – an 'adventure' that the young artist 'demonstrated' before starting her drawing.

F

G

In drawings **G** and **H** the children have shown an interest in depicting the classroom in the background. The child who made drawing **G** shows the ruler which was placed in the crocodile's mouth 'to stop it biting anyone', with the classroom window in the background. The 6-year-old girl who produced drawing **H** shows how she and her friends picked up the crocodile by its tail to throw it out of the room! The child who made drawing **I** has chosen the playground as the location for his crocodile picture in which a comic strip hero grapples with the creature as the child looks on. Detail of the playground furniture, trees and buildings are included in the background landscape.

Going Fishing

Real Objects
Fresh sprats (one for each pair
of children in the class)

❶ Negotiated Drawing

This lesson is designed for a class towards the end of a drawing
programme, who are sufficiently confident about their observational
drawing skills to proceed without the aid of negotiating a drawing
with their teacher.

❷ Developing the Context

Instead of telling a story using words the teacher prepares a mime
which is acted out for the children. At first he signals that he is
hungry, then he picks up a fishing rod, attaches some bait and starts
fishing. After several unsuccessful attempts, he catches a fish and
takes it home where he cooks and eats it! The children share their
interpretation of the mime and their own stories about fishing.

❸ The Children Make Their Own Drawings

A sprat is placed on the table between each pair of children. They are invited to examine these little fish closely and discuss what they look like before the drawing task begins. The children then are asked to either draw their own story about going fishing or to borrow from the teacher's mime in making their picture.

4.9
'Going fishing' – All these drawings were produced by children in Year 2

The boy who made drawing **A** has made up a story about fishing in a pond and shows the fish in the water, with air bubbles drifting to the surface.

A

The girls who made pictures **B** and **C** have made much more detailed drawings of the fish, showing the pattern and texture of the scales. In **B** attention has also been given to the texture of the underwater world.

Note how the boy who produced picture **D** has borrowed the convention of a sequence of drawings, perhaps influenced by 'how to do it' pictures focused upon in an earlier stage of the programme. He may have first-hand experience of going fishing with an adult which could account for the two figures he depicts in his drawing and the detail which he includes about the process of catching a fish.

Daffodils

Real Objects
A bunch of daffodils

 Negotiated Drawing

The teacher selects one large flower as the object for the negotiated drawing with the children.

❷ Developing the Context

This lesson was designed for the later stages of a drawing programme at which point the children were ready to proceed with their own drawings **without the teacher developing an imaginative context for the work.**

❸ The Children Make Their Own Drawings

The teacher places a container of daffodils on each of the tables at which the children are going to work. The children are asked to make a drawing of these flowers without any suggestion of placing them in a fictitious context. However, the teacher does suggest that they might like to draw other children or the classroom in the background.

In drawings **A**, **B** and **C** the children have chosen just to make a carefully observed drawing of the container of daffodils which was placed on their table. In drawing **A** the table has been fitted round the container.

● **4.10**
'Daffodils' – All these drawings were produced by children in Year 1

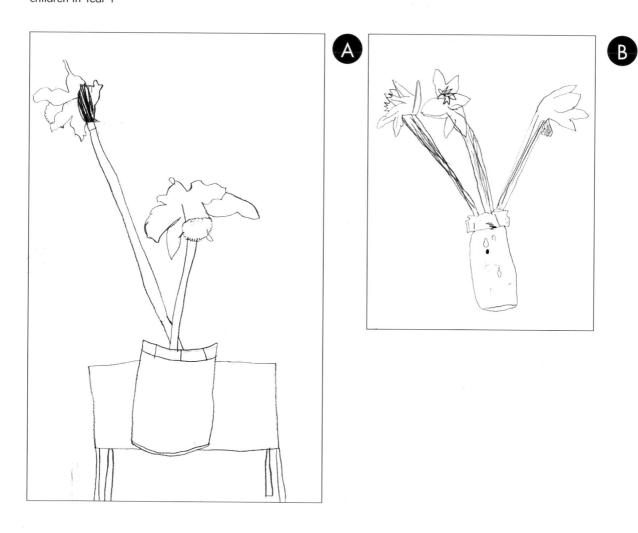

The other drawings show a real interest on the part of the children in depicting the people they can see beyond the container of flowers. In drawing **D** we can see in detail the boy sitting opposite the artist and the drawing which he is in the process of making. The child responsible for drawing I includes a scene across the classroom, with children drawing at different tables and a vacant chair to the top left of the picture.

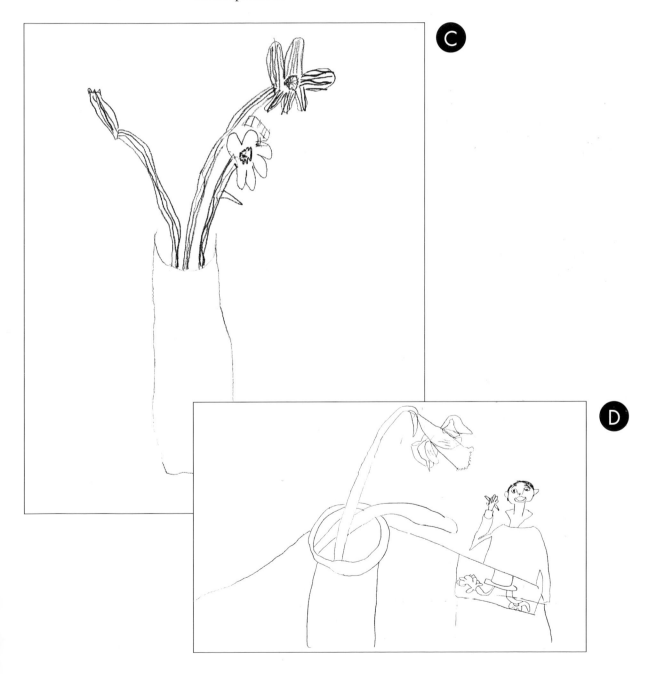

In many cases the drawing of the flowers is very accurate and they could not be mistaken for anything other than daffodils – look in particular at **A**, **B**, **D** and **G**.

In **B**, **G** and **H** particular attention has been paid to the container.

In **A**, **D** and **G** occlusion has been used to indicate relationships between the stalks of the flowers and in **E**, **F** and **G** to place the figures firmly behind the flowers.

Research Findings

'Train and Telegraph Poles', Grant Cooke (1946),
aged 2 years and 9 months.

'Negotiated Drawing' – How Do We Know It Works?

Although teachers may be interested in reading about a different approach to teaching children how to draw they may have reservations about how well it will actually work. They may reasonably argue, why should I use this approach when I'm happy with what I do already? Of course, there's no obligation to change, let alone change to this particular approach. Nevertheless, there are many teachers, both young and old, who have had little or no training or guidance in how to teach art but because of the requirements of the National Curriculum are now having to tackle the issue more earnestly. Although young children have always produced drawings, paintings and other artworks, their teachers have not necessarily given as much thought and attention to them as they have, say, to other school subjects such as reading, writing and number work. The National Curriculum now obliges teachers to give more serious consideration to art for children from the age of 5 to 14 years; indeed, art is one of eight foundation subjects to be taught across this age range. But many teachers feel ill-equipped to cope with this demand. In fact, a recent survey (Clement, 1994) revealed that over 60 per cent of teachers felt the need for further inservice training in order to teach the new art curriculum.

The Need for Objective Evidence

So, does the 'negotiated drawing' approach work? Of course, one way of finding out is to try it and to see if it works for you. Many teachers operate on this intuitive and personal basis. If the children's experiences and the resulting drawings seem to confirm our expectations then we are content to carry on. But other teachers may seek more objective confirmation before continuing with an approach or even trying it out at all. It was with this goal in mind – seeking objective validation – that we set about devising a research study to evaluate the 'negotiated drawing' approach.

Evaluating the Drawings

Of course, this raises a further question: What exactly are we trying to evaluate? One person may be primarily concerned with the interactional processes involved when the children 'help' the teacher to produce a graphic image, another may be more concerned with the imaginative and dramatic aspects of a lesson, and yet another may be focused on the actual drawings produced by the children. Many teachers will value all of these aspects as part of a holistic approach, as indeed was the intention when the 'negotiated drawing' approach was first devised. For the purposes of our evaluation study, however, we decided to concentrate on the children's own drawings. This is not to deny the importance of the other aspects of the approach nor to relegate them to some lesser status, but we felt that the drawings are, to a large extent, the 'public trace' of the children's experience in the lessons. As such, they are more accessible to objective evaluation and also represented tangible evidence of one of the goals of the exercise – children's improved skill in drawing from a model in an imaginative way.

Even when we focus on the drawings themselves, however, we are still faced with the issue of what exactly it is that we are evaluating. Is it the quality of line, the boldness of the picture, its detail, the composition of the scene, all of these things, or something else? Should we focus on the idea or 'conception' of the picture rather than be considering the child's technical ability to draw? We ran some 'pilot' studies to see if adults can separate out these issues. We asked some researchers familiar with children's developing ability to draw to evaluate a set of drawings all on the same topic drawn by 5- to 7-year-olds. First, we asked them to judge each picture according to its technical skill and, next, on how imaginative and expressive it was. In general, a technically good picture was also judged to be good in terms of imaginative expression. Similarly a technically poor picture was judged to be imaginatively poor too. Whereas we sometimes hear the criticism that an adolescent or adult's picture can be technically proficient but that the idea and the interpretation are poor, it was difficult to make this kind of distinction with these young children's drawings. It may be that these criteria are not separable when applied to the drawings of very young artists. As a result of this 'pilot' testing we decided to judge the children's pictures in a holistic way, that is simply to allow judges to use their own intuitive criteria and to assess each drawing on a poor–excellent rating scale.

'Before' and 'After' Drawings

When evaluating a change over a particular period of time it is necessary to find out what the children's level is at the beginning, find out the level at the end and then compare the two. In fact, a standard research technique is to give the children the same drawing task at the beginning of the study and then again at the end so that we can see more directly whether or not the later drawings are an improvement on the earlier ones. We might not expect *every* child to improve nor everyone to improve equally but, in order for us to claim success for our approach, we would want to see a significant improvement in the average performance of a group of children.

We asked the children to complete some drawings at the beginning and then again at the end of our study. Here, we shall discuss only one of these 'before' and 'after' drawing tasks (for the interested reader a fuller account of our research study is available elsewhere (Cox, Eames and Cooke, 1994; Cox, Cooke and Griffin, 1995)): each child was seen individually and was asked to observe a toy version of a dial-telephone and to draw it; the telephone remained in position throughout this 'still-life' task. So, the child's task was simply to observe the object and make a representational drawing.

Comparing Different Approaches

How can we know if an improvement in drawing skill over time is actually due to our negotiated drawing approach or is simply a 'normal' developmental change? The way we solved this problem was to compare the children tutored by the negotiated drawing approach with another group who were taught over the same period of time in a 'normal' way. What do we mean by 'normal'? There are many ways that teachers teach, probably as many as there are teachers. But a common way that teachers of young children teach art is to tell a story or incident, often related to an ongoing classroom project, or to use interesting or dramatic objects as stimuli. Stories or objects are used to create a context and inspire the children's imagination. But the teacher rarely focuses on the process of observation of objects or on the drawing process itself. It is this attention to the way in which objects can be observed and shapes can be 'extracted' which distinguishes the negotiated drawing approach. So, we contrasted this approach with what we called, for want of a better term, a 'normal' approach.

Teachers might well feel that the negotiated drawing approach may work for someone who is an art specialist – someone who is a capable artist and who is also committed to this particular approach – and that the success of the approach owes more to the ability and enthusiasm of that particular person than to the approach itself. In order to test this possibility we decided to compare four groups of children. The first group received a set of lessons taught by the first author of this book, Grant Cooke. The second group received exactly the same set of lessons taught by a supply teacher who was not an art specialist. If the approach is to be recommended to others then we must demonstrate that it is effective even when taught by an 'ordinary' teacher. The third group of children received the same number of lessons on the same topics, but they were taught by Grant Cooke using a 'normal' teaching approach, that is using the same objects and scene-setting devices but omitting the attention to the drawing process itself. Finally, a fourth group of children received lessons from their class teachers along these lines.

Four schools agreed to participate in our research study. They each contributed two classes of children. We randomly allocated these classes to our four teaching 'conditions', with the proviso that no school could contribute both classes to any one condition. The table below shows, for each teaching condition, the total number of children, numbers of boys and girls, and details of their ages.

Number of children in each teaching condition

Teaching condition	1 Negotiated drawing Grant Cooke	2 Negotiated drawing Supply teacher	3 Normal teaching Grant Cooke	4 Normal teaching Class teachers
Teacher				
No. of boys	30	27	30	29
No. of girls	32	27	28	32
Total	62	54	58	61
Average age	5;10	5;9	5;10	5;9
Age range	5;4–6;3	5;3–7;0	5;4–6;11	5;3-6;3

Equal at the Start

It was important to establish that the children in the four conditions were as similar as possible in both their general ability and in their drawing skill, otherwise any differences that we might find at the end of the study could be attributed to differences that were already there at the beginning. First of all, we tested all the children individually on the Raven's Coloured Progressive Matrices which assesses non-verbal reasoning. Next, we asked them to draw a person and then scored these figures according to the Goodenough-Harris scoring system and also the Koppitz system. There is evidence that the scores children achieve in this way correlate fairly well with their intellectual maturity. We also asked the children, again individually, what they felt about their own drawing ability and we asked them to point to one of a set of four cartoon faces (from glum, indicating 'very poor at drawing', to smiling broadly, indicating 'very good at drawing'). There were no statistically significant differences among the children in the four conditions on any of these measures. As we shall see later, there were also no significant differences on the telephone drawings either, so we were satisfied that at the beginning of the study the four groups were starting off on an equal footing.

The Ten Drawing Lessons

We devised a programme of ten drawing lessons for all four 'conditions' and these were given over a five-week period. Each lesson had a different topic. The same ten topics (topics included in this book) were used in three conditions but the class teachers in condition 4 used only two of these topics; their other eight lessons were topics of their own choice. Consequently it was possible to make direct comparisons across the four conditions only on two drawing topics – 'A Magic Bicycle' and 'Daffodils'.

The Judges

We asked three former art advisers to judge the pictures. They had all had special responsibility for training and advising teachers of young children and also had worked with young children themselves. Although formally retired, these advisers were continuing with part-time work in their field.

Judges' Ratings

We number-coded each drawing and randomized the order within each task (we shall call them 'telephone', 'bicycle' and 'daffodil' drawings). So, for example, all the 'before' and 'after' telephone drawings produced by all the children in the study were completely jumbled up in one set. The judges knew the age-range of the children and the instructions they had been given. But, apart from that, they had no knowledge of the 'condition' a drawing belonged to and they were not told that there had been a 'before' and an 'after' drawing for the telephone topic. The judges took one topic at a time and were asked to sort the drawings into five piles: 1) very poor, 2) below average, 3) average, 4) quite good, 5) excellent. They were encouraged to re-assess each pile until they were quite satisfied with their judgements. Each judge rated the drawings separately and independently.

As we explained earlier, we did not give the judges **specific** criteria by which to rate the pictures and one might wonder whether there would be any similarity at all in their judgments. In fact, the agreement among the three of them was very high. Ninety per cent of the 'telephone' drawings were given exactly the same rating by all three judges **or** the same rating by two judges with the third judge only one category rating apart. Similarly, the judges' agreement for the other sets of drawings were 82 per cent for the 'bicycle' drawings and 90 per cent for the 'daffodils'. Clearly, the judges must have been using similar criteria even though we didn't specify any and when we asked them to reflect on and write down their criteria they did indeed mention similar things. They said they had looked for a vital sense of the object in question, the shape of its different parts and their interrelationships, the amount of detail, proportions, composition, representation of occlusion, three-dimensionality, and the maturity, confidence and originality of the drawing.

The Results of the Study

We gave each drawing in the 'very poor' pile a rating of 1, each drawing in the 'below average' pile a rating of 2, and so on up to a rating of 5 for the 'excellent' drawings. In this way each drawing received a quantitative value from 1 to 5 from each judge. The three judges' ratings for that drawing were then averaged. The two 'bicycle' drawings (figure 5.1) will give you an idea of the kinds of picture which received very low and very high ratings. The upper picture, drawn by a child in condition 1, received ratings of 1; whereas the lower picture, drawn by a child in condition 2, received ratings of 5. Similarly, the upper drawings of daffodils (figure 5.1) was rated 1 and the lower was rated 5; both drawers were in condition 4. We should point out that the reason for allocating a numerical value to the drawings was for the purposes of statistical analysis of the data within a research study; we are not advocating this as normal practice within a teaching context.

● **5.1**
The magic bicycle drawing at the top received ratings of 1 and the one at the bottom received ratings of 5 from the judges.

● **5.2**
The daffodil drawing at the top received ratings of 1 and the one at the bottom received ratings of 5 from the judges.

So, let's see what ratings the children in the four conditions received for their bicycle and daffodil drawings. We can see from the histograms below that the children who were taught by Grant Cooke (condition 1) and the supply teacher (condition 2) using the negotiated drawing approach received on average higher ratings for their drawings from the judges than did children who were taught in a 'normal' way (conditions 3 and 4).

Now, let's look at the judges' ratings of the telephone drawings. The

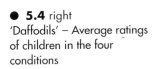

● **5.3** left
'A Magic Bicycle' – Average ratings of children in the four conditions

● **5.4** right
'Daffodils' – Average ratings of children in the four conditions

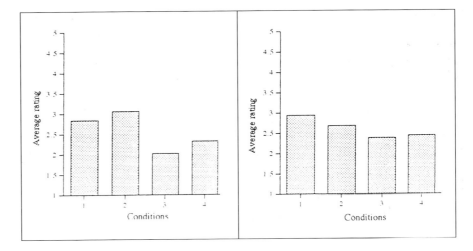

children in all four conditions received similar average ratings for the drawings they did at the start of the study; statistically, there was no significant difference among them. But we can see from the histogram (figure 5.5) that the 'after' drawings in each condition were rated more highly on average than the 'before' drawings; this is not surprising since all the children were getting older, gaining in experience and having art lessons. What we particularly want to know is whether the children in the negotiated drawing conditions (conditions 1 and 2) received higher ratings for their 'after' drawings than the children in the other two conditions (conditions 3 and 4). Statistical analyses carried out on the ratings confirm that this was indeed the case. The upper drawing of a telephone (figure 5.6) was produced by a child in condition 1; it received ratings of 1 and 2 from the judges. After being taught by the negotiated drawing approach, the same child produced the lower picture at the end of the study; this drawing received ratings of 3 and 4 from the judges.

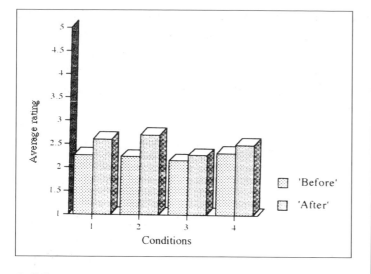

● **5.5**
'Telephone' – 'Before' and 'After' ratings of children in the four conditions

● **5.6**
A 6-year-old boy's drawing of a telephone before (top) and after (below) the programme of 'negotiated drawing' lessons

Conclusion

This research study provides us with evidence that the negotiated drawing approach leads to improved ratings for children's drawings. This is the case not only for those drawings completed during the lessons themselves (the bicycle and daffodil drawings) but also for a 'test' topic (the telephone drawings) for which no special tuition had been involved. This suggests that the observational and drawing skills that the children acquire in their negotiated drawing lessons will generalize to other drawing topics.

The study also shows that the negotiated drawing approach works for a non-specialist teacher as well as for an art specialist; the supply teacher who took part in this study certainly did not consider herself at all good at art but she was enthusiastic about the approach. This finding is important since most teachers of young children are non-specialists and as a recent survey has revealed (Clement, 1994) many feel poorly qualified to fulfil the requirements of the National Curriculum in Art.

Finally, we wish to stress that the negotiated drawing approach does not mean that children are taught a rigid formula for drawing objects. Nor are they indoctrinated into one particular way of drawing. Through discussion they are encouraged to look at objects closely and to think about their shapes and proportions but the way they then choose to represent those objects is left to their own imaginations. We believe that the way that the negotiated drawing approach embeds observation of an object in an interesting and often dramatic context is a fruitful way of teaching representational drawing. This should be advantageous not only in improving children's artwork but also their drawings used for recording and understanding material in other areas of the school curriculum.

The gains made by the children in our research study are significant but modest. This is not surprising since the research programme consisted of only ten lessons given over a five-week period. We predict that if these children were regularly to be taught with the negotiated drawing approach then their drawings would improve even further. As Pariser (1979, p. 40) has argued:

> ...it takes much practice to develop skill in using a medium to match one's visual experience. Thus, training in the service of a medium is central to the task of maintaining vital, personal expression. Without knowledgeable seeing and skilled use of media no child can give full vent to his or her own feelings and concerns.

References

Alland, A. (1983) *Playing with Form*, New York: Columbia University Press.

Belo, J. (1955) 'Balinese children's drawings', In Mead, M. and Wolfenstein, M. (Eds) *Childhood in Contemporary Cultures*, Chicago: Chicago University Press.

Calouste Gulbenkian Foundation (1982) *The Arts in Schools*, Calouste Gulbenkian Foundation.

Clement, R. (1994) 'The readiness of primary schools to teach the National Curriculum in Art and Design', *Journal of Art and Design Education*, **13**, 9–19.

Cox, M.V. (1992) *Children's Drawings*, Harmondsworth, Middx.: Penguin Books.

Cox, M.V. (1993) *Children's Drawings of the Human Figure*, Hove, UK & Hillsdale, USA: Lawrence Erlbaum.

Cox, M.V., Cooke, G. and Griffin, D. (1995) 'Teaching children to draw in the Infants School', *Journal of Art and Design Education*, **14**, 153–163.

Cox, M.V., Eames, K. and Cooke, G. (1994) 'The teaching of drawing in the Infants school: An evaluation of the "negotiated drawing" approach', *International Journal of Early Years Education*, **2**, 68–83.

Cox, M.V. and Hill, R. (1996) 'Different strokes', *The Times Higher Educational Supplement*, 9 August.

DES (1983) *9–13 Middle Schools: An illustrative survey*, London: HMSO.

DES (1990) *Interim Report of the National Curriculum Art Working Group*, London: HMSO.

DES (1991) *Art for Ages 5 to 14*, London: HMSO.

Department for Education (1995) *Art in the National Curriculum*, London: HMSO.

Donaldson, M. (1978) *Children's Minds*, Glasgow: Fontana/Collins.

Edwards, B. (1979) *Drawing on the Right Side of the Brain*, Los Angeles: Tarcher.

Edwards, B. (1986) *Drawing on the Artist Within*, Glasgow: Fontana/Collins. Los Angeles: Tarcher.

Fortes, M. (1940) 'Children's drawings among the Tallensi', *Africa*, **13**, 239–295.

Fortes, M. (1981) 'Tallensi children's drawings', in Lloyd, B. and Gay, J. (Eds) *Universals of Human Thought*, Cambridge: Cambridge University Press.

Freeman, N.H. (1980) *Strategies of Representation in Young Children*, London: Academic Press.

Gombrich, E.H. (1980) *Art and Illusion* (5th edition), London: Phaidon Press.

Löwenfeld, V. (1957) *Creative and Mental Growth* (3rd edition), New York: Macmillan.

Pariser, D.A. (1979) 'Two methods of teaching drawing skills', *Studies in Art Education*, **20**, 30–42.

Pemberton, E.F. and Nelson, K.E. (1987) 'Using interactive graphic challenges to foster young children's drawing ability', *Visual Arts Research*, **13**, 29–41.

Rushdie, S. (1990) 'In good faith', *The Independent*, 4 February.

Vygotsky, L.S. (1934/62) *Thought and Language*, Cambridge, Ma.: MIT Press.

Wilson, B. (1985) 'The artistic tower of Babel: Inextricable links between culture and graphic development', *Visual Arts Research*, **11**, 90–104.